PIANO - VOCAL - GUITAR

the twilight saga
new moon

MUSIC FROM THE MOTION PICTURE SOUNDTRACK

SUMMIT ENTERTAINMENT PRESENTS "THE TWILIGHT SAGA: NEW MOON"

A TEMPLE HILL PRODUCTION IN ASSOCIATION WITH MAVERICK/IMPRINT AND SUNSWEPT ENTERTAINMENT KRISTEN STEWART ROBERT PATTINSON TAYLOR LAUTNER ASHLEY GREENE RACHELLE LEFEVRE BILLY BURKE PETER FACINELLI ELIZABETH REASER NIKKI REED KELLAN LUTZ JACKSON RATHBONE ANNA KENDRICK WITH MICHAEL SHEEN AND DAKOTA FANNING CASTING BY JOSEPH MIDDLETON, C.S.A. MUSIC BY ALEXANDRE DESPLAT MUSIC SUPERVISOR ALEXANDRA PATSAVAS COSTUME DESIGNER TISH MONAGHAN EDITOR PETER LAMBERT PRODUCTION DESIGNER DAVID BRISBIN DIRECTOR OF PHOTOGRAPHY JAVIER AGUIRRESAROBE CO-PRODUCER BILL BANNERMAN EXECUTIVE PRODUCERS MARTY BOWEN GREG MOORADIAN MARK MORGAN GUY OSEARY PRODUCED BY WYCK GODFREY KAREN ROSENFELT BASED ON THE NOVEL "NEW MOON" BY STEPHENIE MEYER

PG-13 PARENTS STRONGLY CAUTIONED
Some Material May Be Inappropriate for Children Under 13
Some Violence and Action

11.20.09

SCREENPLAY BY MELISSA ROSENBERG DIRECTED BY CHRIS WEITZ

Original Motion Film Soundtrack Available On Atlantic Records

www.newmoonthemovie.com

ISBN 978-1-4234-8992-4

HAL•LEONARD®
CORPORATION
7777 W. BLUEMOUND RD. P.O. BOX 13819 MILWAUKEE, WI 53213

MEET ME ON THE EQUINOX

Words and Music by BENJAMIN GIBBARD,
CHRISTOPHER WALLA, NICHOLAS HARMER
and JASON McGERR

Moderate Rock

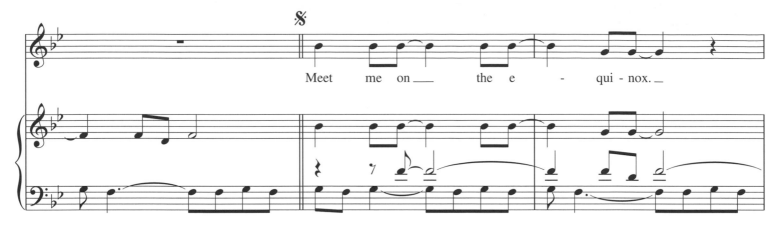

Meet me on __ the e - qui - nox. __

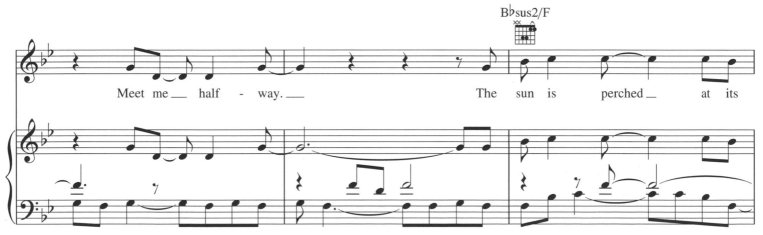

Meet me __ half - way. __ The sun is perched __ at its

high - est peak __ in the mid - dle of __ the day. __

Let me give — my love — to you, — let me take your hand. —

Bbsus2/F

And as we walk — in the dim-ming light, — oh

G7(no3)

dar - ling un - der - stand — that ev - 'ry - thing,

To Coda ✛ **Eb**

Cm7

ev - 'ry - thing ends, —

G7(no3)

That

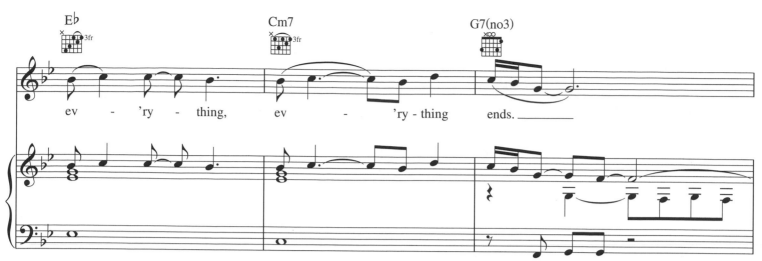

ev - 'ry - thing, ev - 'ry-thing ends. _____

Meet me on ___ your best ___ be - hav - ior, meet me at your worst. __

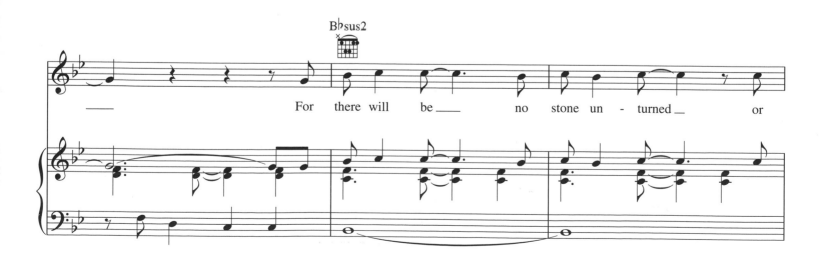

___ For there will be ___ no stone un - turned ___ or

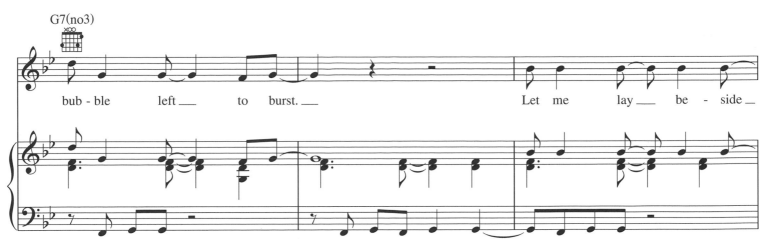

bub - ble left ___ to burst. ___ Let me lay ___ be - side ___

___ you dar - ling, let me be your man ___ and

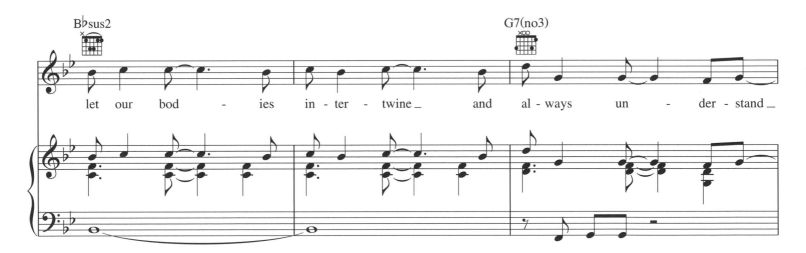

let our bod - ies in - ter - twine ___ and al - ways un - der - stand ___

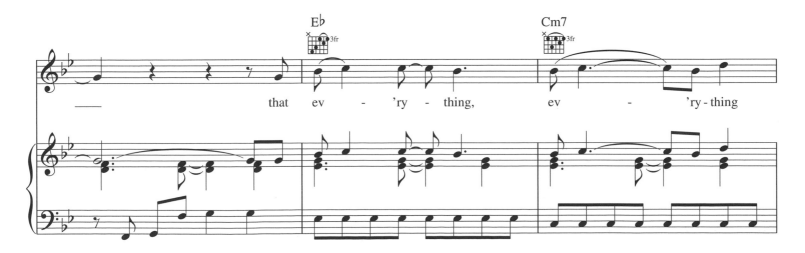

that ev - 'ry - thing, ev - 'ry - thing

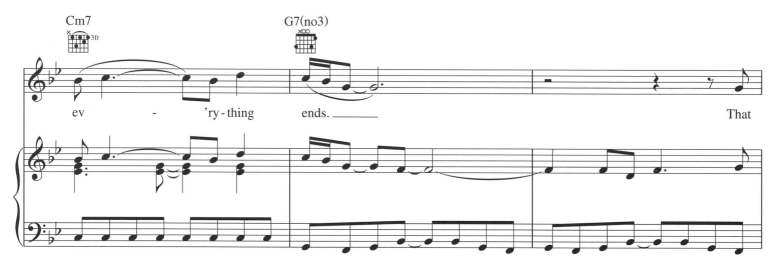

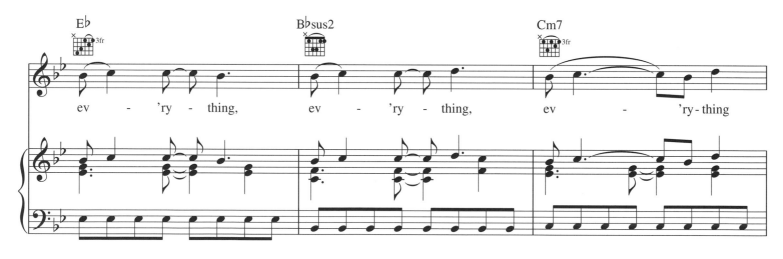

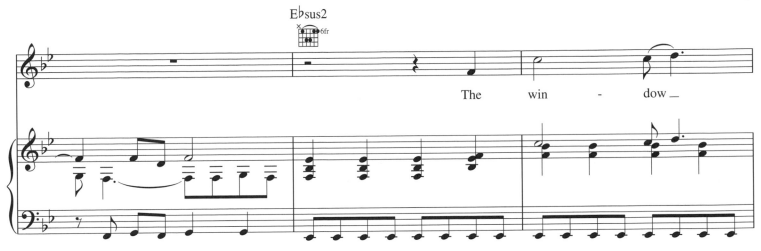

The win- dow ___

can o- pen ___ too. ___ The

sun crawls ___ a- cross your bed- room.

The ha- lo, ___ the

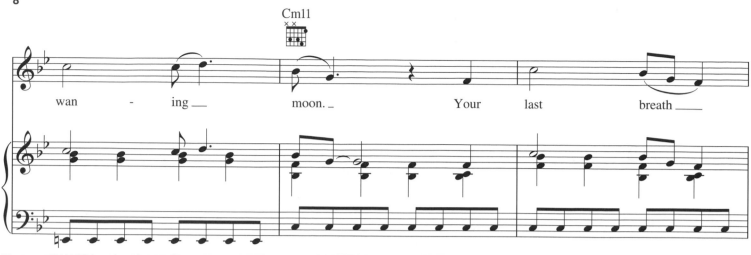

wan - ing ___ moon. ___ Your last breath ___

mov - ing through ___ you as ev - 'ry - thing,

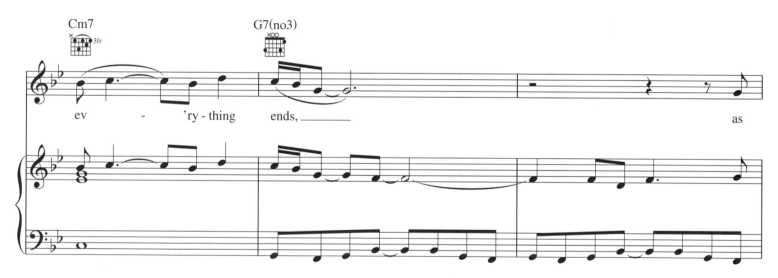

ev - 'ry - thing ends, ___ as

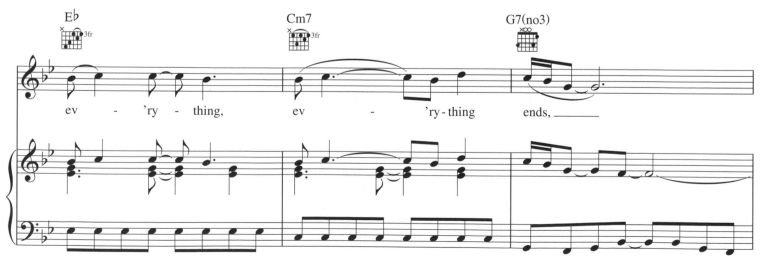

ev - 'ry - thing, ev - 'ry - thing ends, ___

as ev - 'ry - thing,   ev - 'ry - thing,

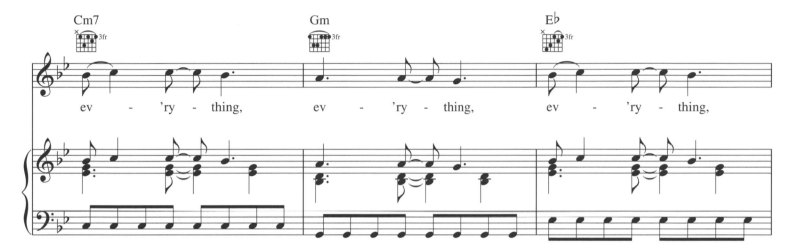

ev - 'ry - thing,   ev - 'ry - thing,   ev - 'ry - thing,

ev - 'ry - thing   ends. _____

Play 3 times
then D.S. al Coda

CODA

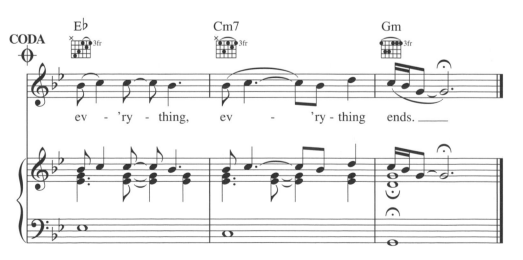

ev - 'ry - thing,   ev - 'ry - thing   ends. _____

FRIENDS

Words and Music by RUSSELL MARSDEN,
EMMA RICHARDSON and MATTHEW HAYWARD

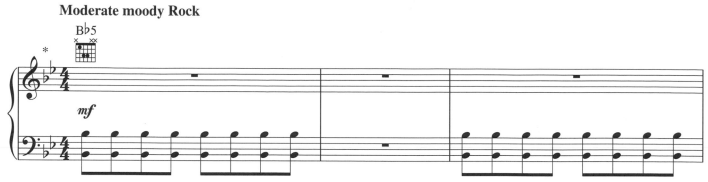

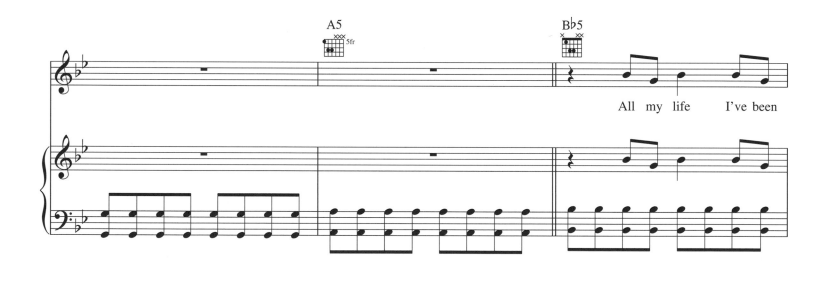

All my life I've been

search-in' for some-thin', _ some-thin' I can put my fin-ger on. _

* *Recorded a half step higher.*

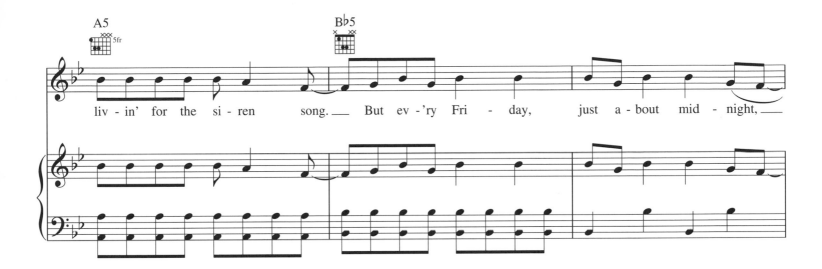

love 'cause on - ly love is true.__ I need ev - 'ry wak - in'

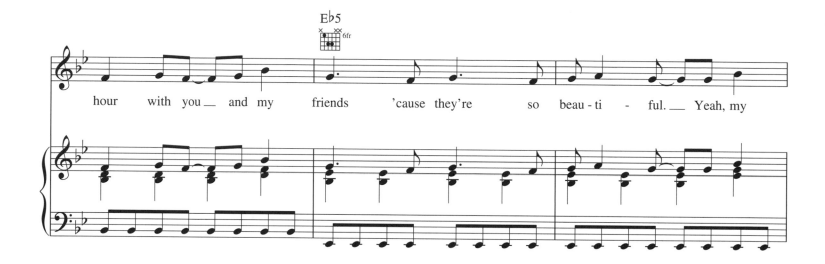

hour with you__ and my friends 'cause they're so beau - ti - ful.__ Yeah, my

friends they are so beau - ti - ful.__ They're my friends.

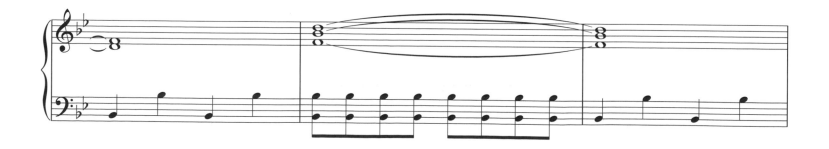

All my life I've been wast-in',___ wast-in'.___

Wast-in' all my mon-ey, all___ my time.___ All the time that I'm

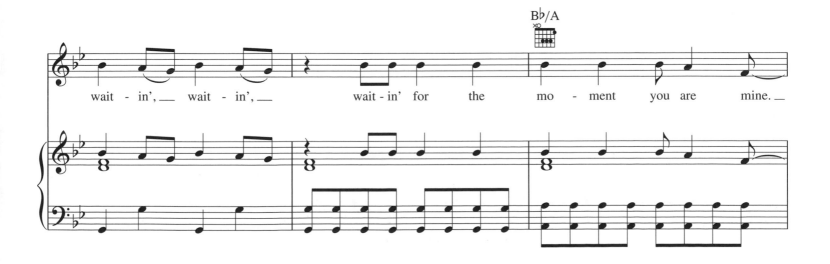

wait-in',___ wait-in',___ wait-in' for the mo-ment you are mine.___

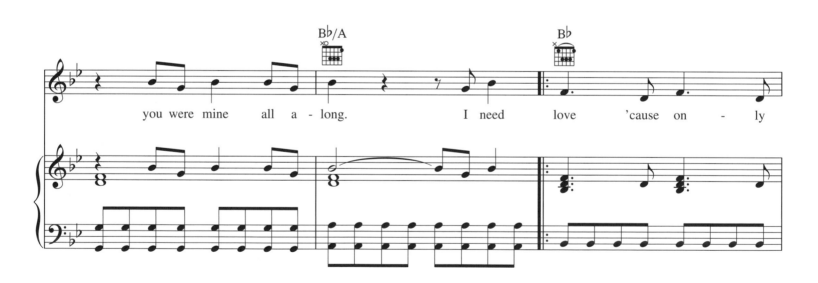

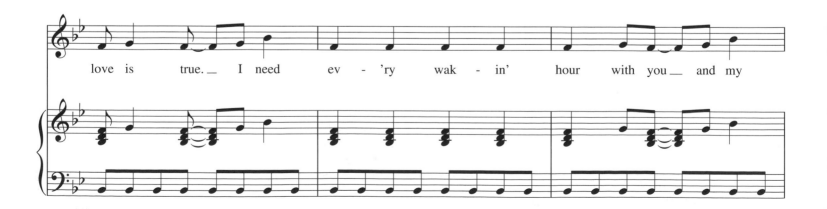

friends 'cause they're so beau-ti - ful. __ Yeah, my friends they are so beau-ti - ful. __ { I need
They're my

friends.   friends
                    (On repeat only.)   They're my

friends.   They're my   friends.   They're my

friends.   They're my   friends.

HEARING DAMAGE

Words and Music by
THOM YORKE

Moderate Techno groove

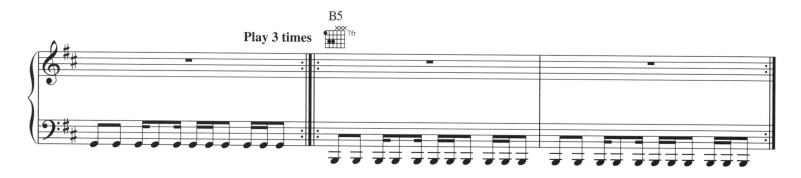

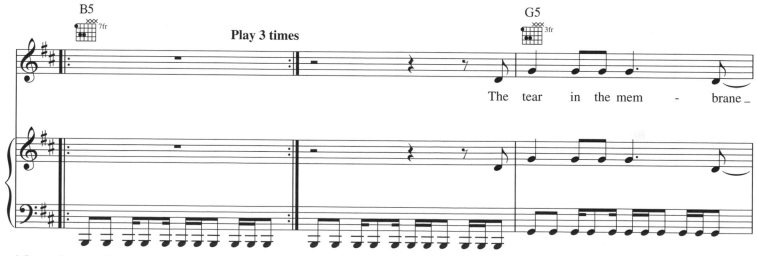

The tear in the mem - brane

* Recorded a half step lower.

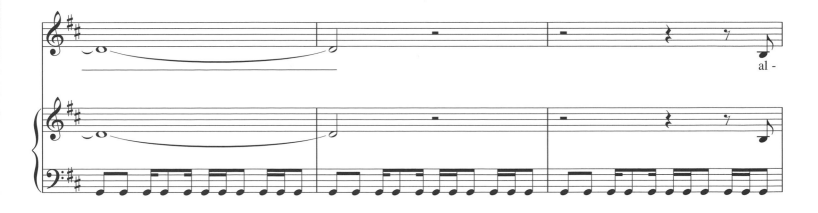

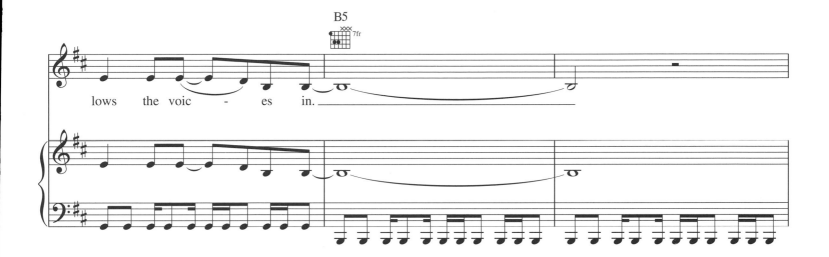

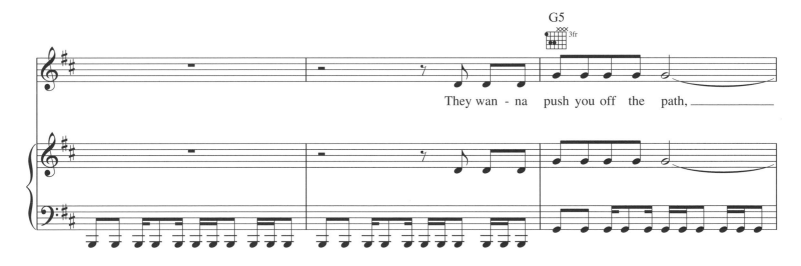

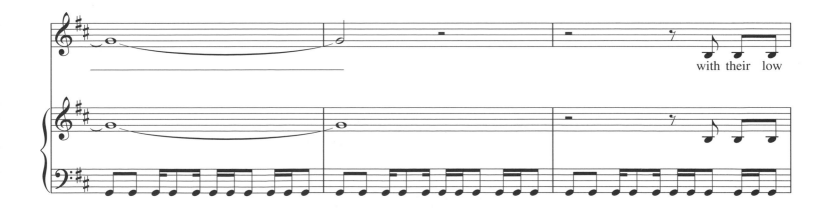

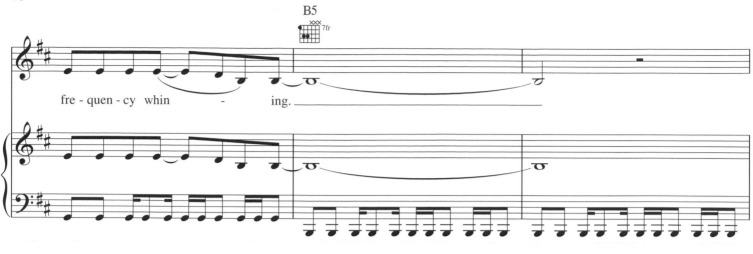

fre - quen - cy whin - ing.

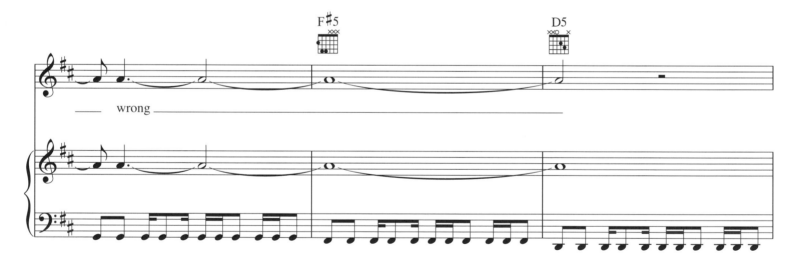

You can do ___ no ___

___ wrong

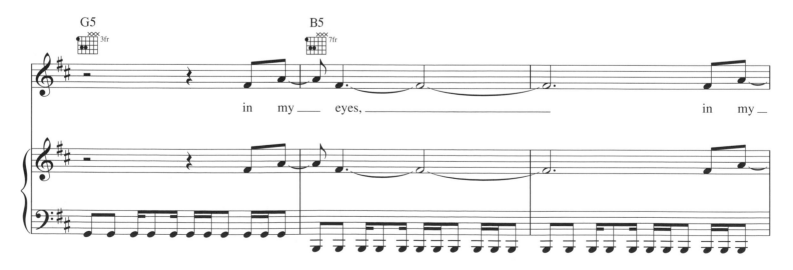

in my ___ eyes, ___ in my ___

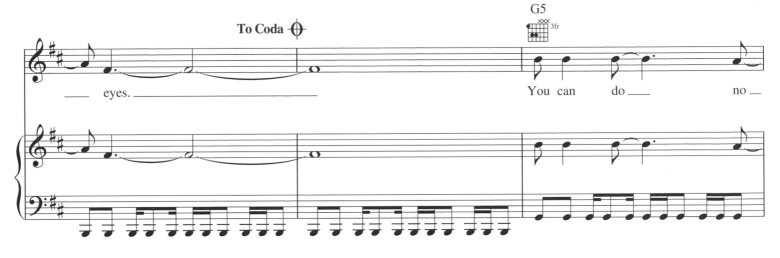

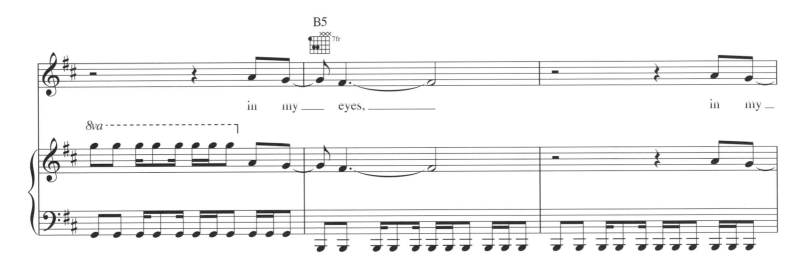

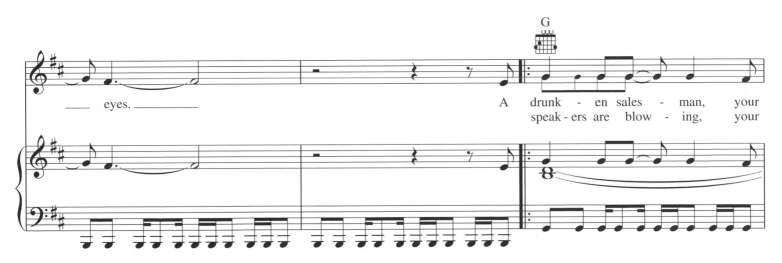

hear - ing dam - age. Your mind is rest - less. They say you're get - ting bet - ter but
ears are wreck - ing. Your hear - ing dam - age. You wish you felt __ bet - ter. You

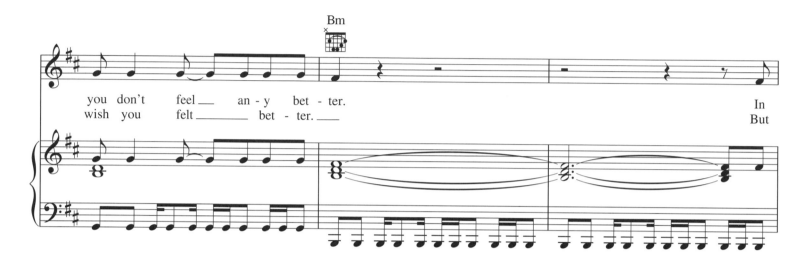

you don't feel __ an - y bet - ter.
wish you felt __ bet - ter. __

In
But

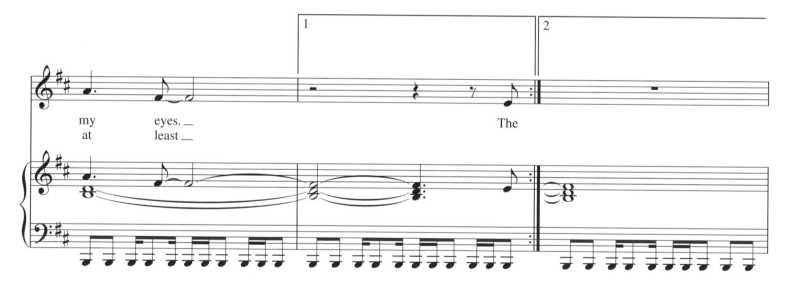

my eyes. __
at least __

The

you can do __ no __ wrong _____

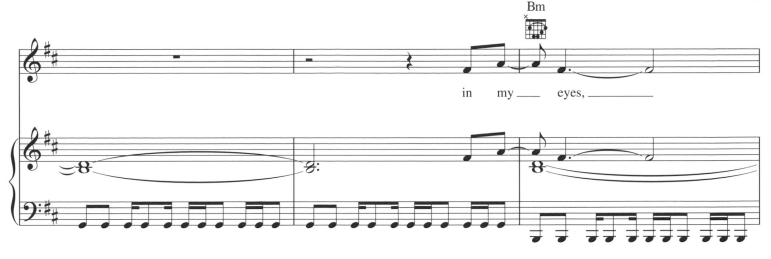

in my ___ eyes, _____

D.S. al Coda

in my ___ eyes. _____

CODA

___ In my ___ eyes. _____

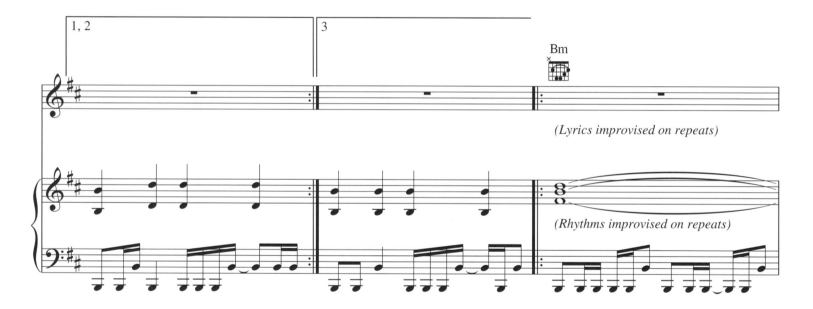

(Lyrics improvised on repeats)

(Rhythms improvised on repeats)

Repeat 12 times

POSSIBILITY

Words and Music by
LYKKE LI ZACHRISSON

Slow, moody ballad

There's a pos - si - bil - i - ty. _____
Know that when _ you ____ leave. _____

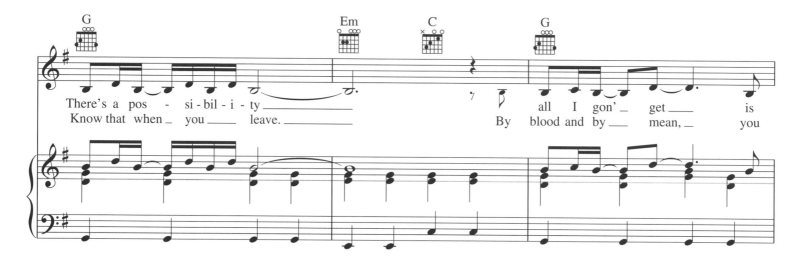

There's a pos - si - bil - i - ty _____ all I gon' get ____ is
Know that when _ you ____ leave. _____ By blood and by _ mean, _ you

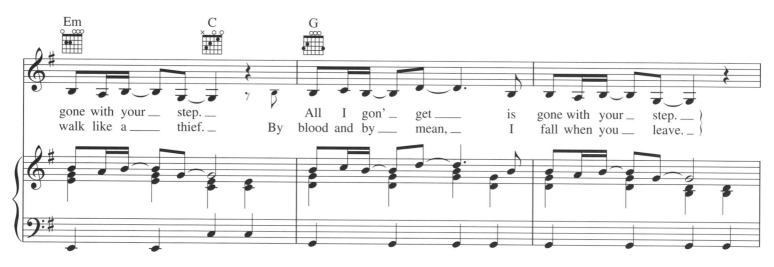

gone with your _ step. _ All I gon' get ____ is gone with your _ step. _
walk like a ____ thief. _ By blood and by _ mean, _ I fall when you _ leave. _

So tell me when you hear my heart ____ stop. ____

You're the on - ly one who knows. ___ Tell me when you hear my si -

- lence. ___ There's a pos - si - bil - i - ty ___ I would-n't

know, umm, ___

umm. ___

So tell me when my sigh is ov - er. _____

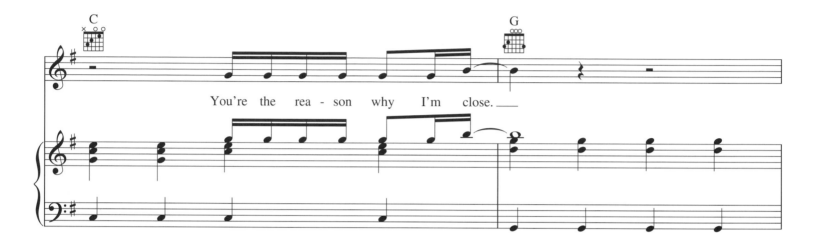

You're the rea - son why I'm close. _____

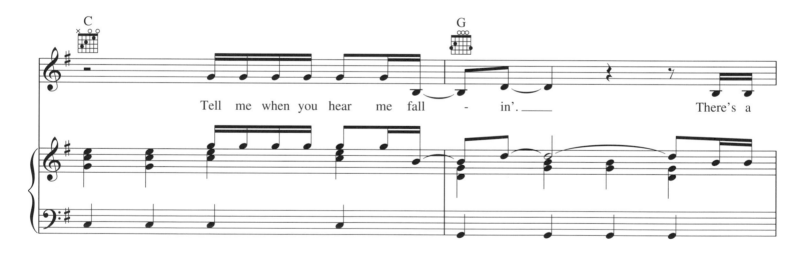

Tell me when you hear me fall - in'. _____ There's a

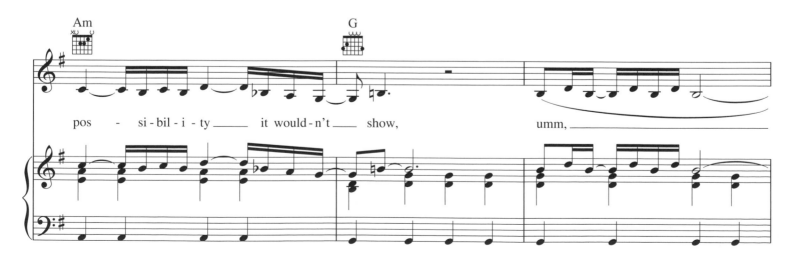

pos - si - bil - i - ty _____ it would - n't _____ show, umm, _____

umm. _____ By

blood and by ___ mean, ___ I fall when you ___ leave. ___ By blood and by ___ mean, ___ I'll

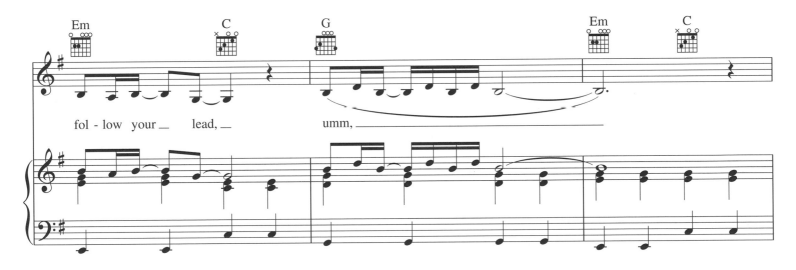

fol - low your ___ lead, ___ umm, _____

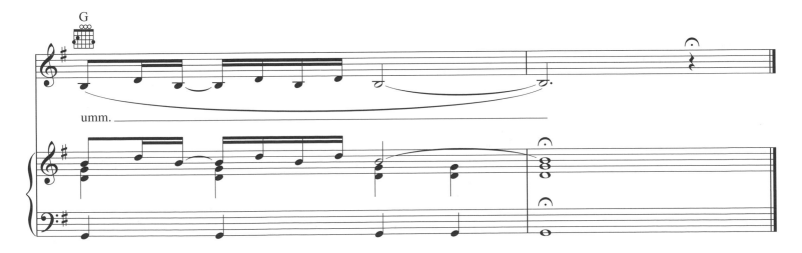

umm. _____

A WHITE DEMON LOVE SONG

Words and Music by
THE KILLERS

White de - mon love song down the hall.

Recorded a half step higher.

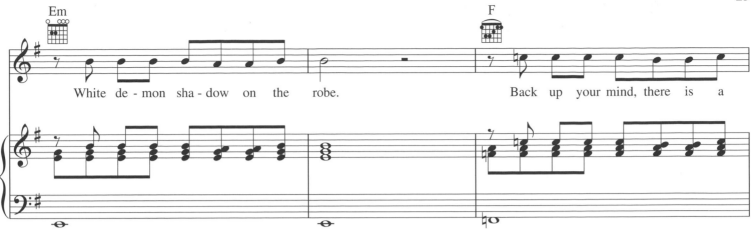

White de-mon sha-dow on the robe. Back up your mind, there is a

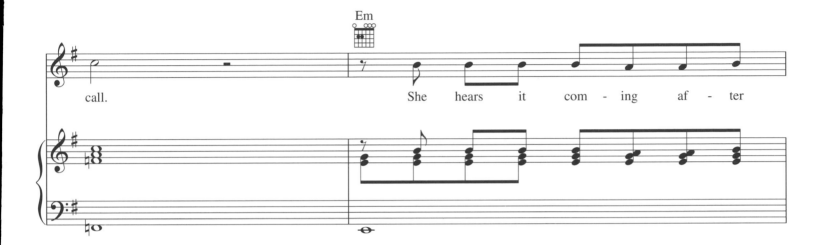

call. She hears it com-ing af-ter

all of this time. ___ She likes _ the way _ he sings

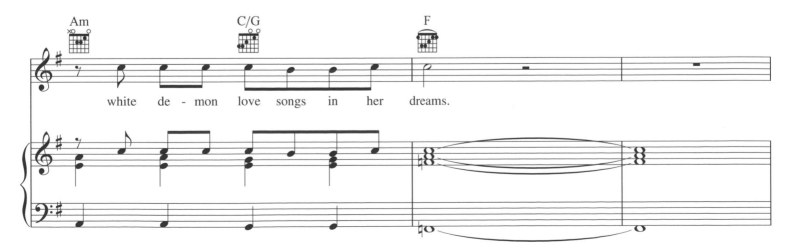

white de-mon love songs in her dreams.

White de-mon, where's your self-ish kiss? White de-mon sor-row will ar-

range. Let's not for-get a-bout the fear. _____

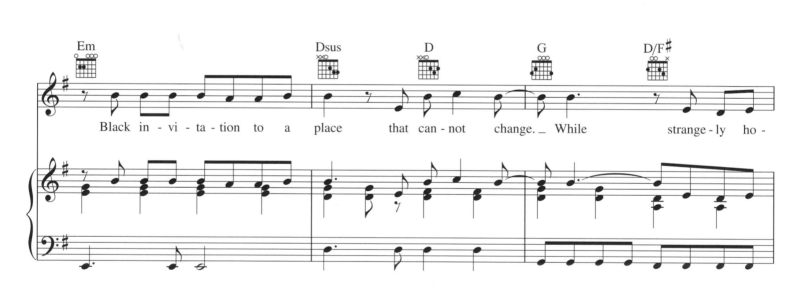

Black in-vi-ta-tion to a place that can-not change. _ While strange-ly ho-

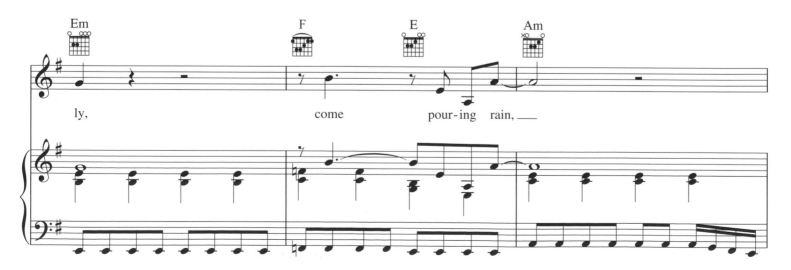

ly, come pour-ing rain, ___

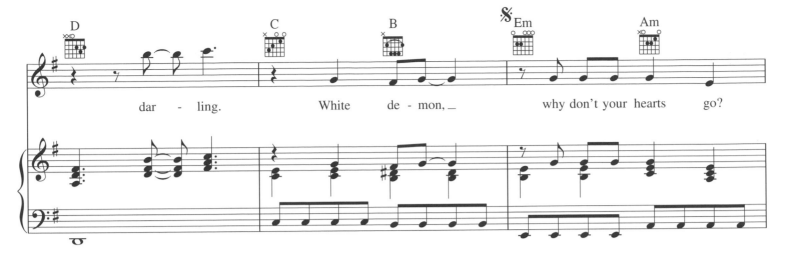

dar - ling. White de - mon, — why don't your hearts go?

White de - mon, — who let your friend go? — White de - mon, —

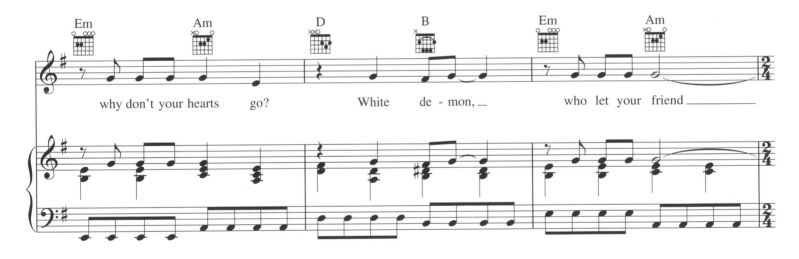

why don't your hearts go? White de - mon, — who let your friend _____

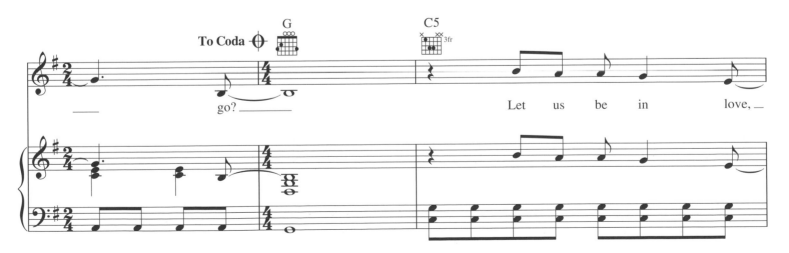

__ go? __ Let us be in love, __

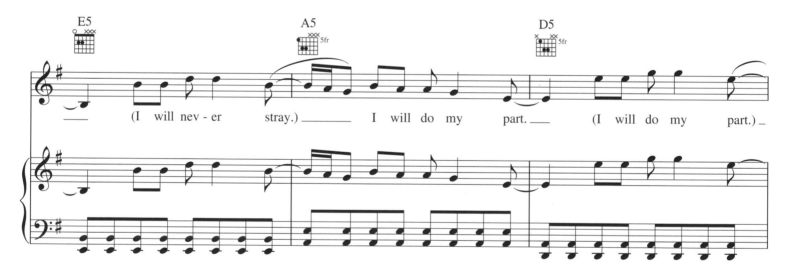

CODA

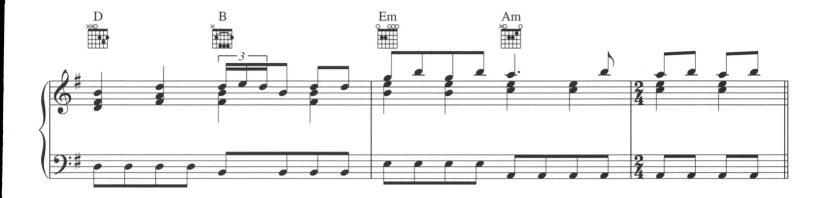

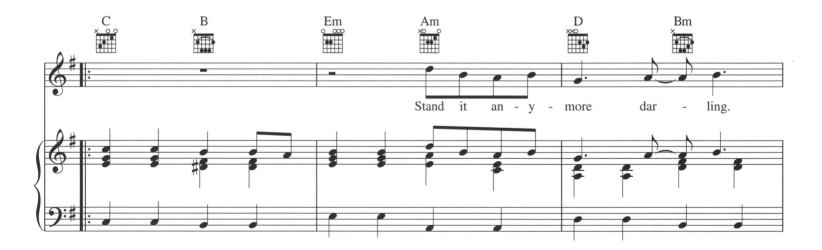

Stand it an - y - more dar - ling.

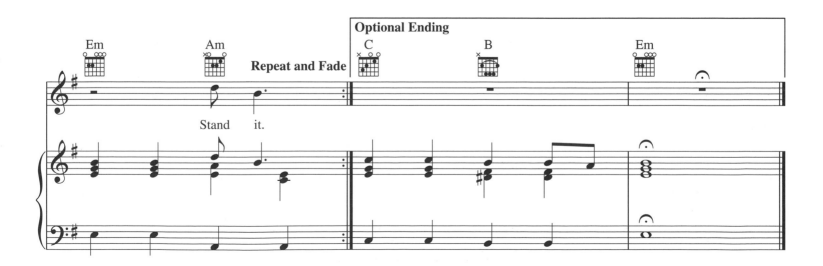

Optional Ending

Repeat and Fade

Stand it.

SATELLITE HEART

Words and Music by
ANYA MARINA

So pret-ty, so smart. ___ Such a

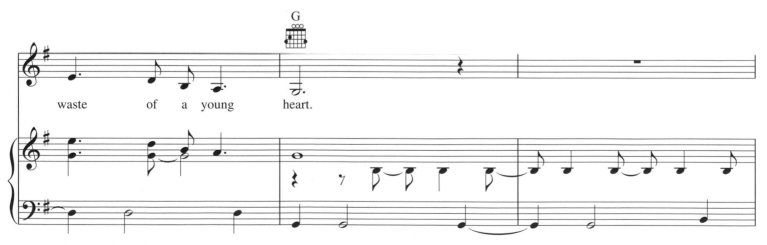

waste of a young heart.

Recorded a half step lower.

What a pi - ty. What a sham. __ What's the

mat - ter with __ you man? __

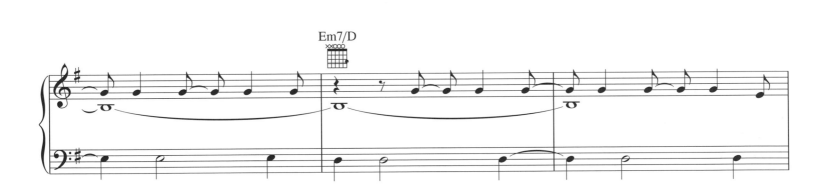

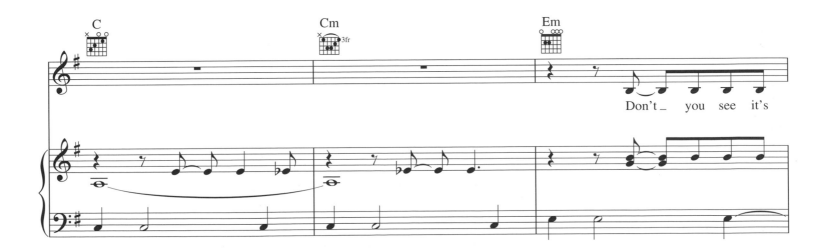

Don't __ you see it's

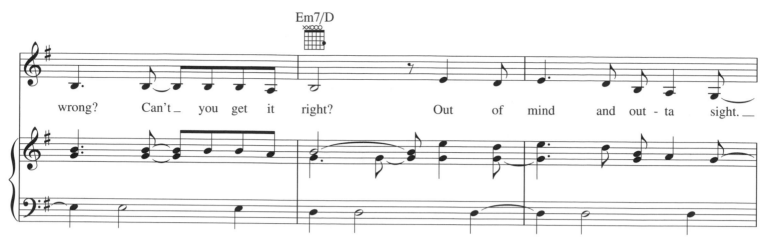

wrong? Can't _ you get it right? Out of mind and out - ta sight. _

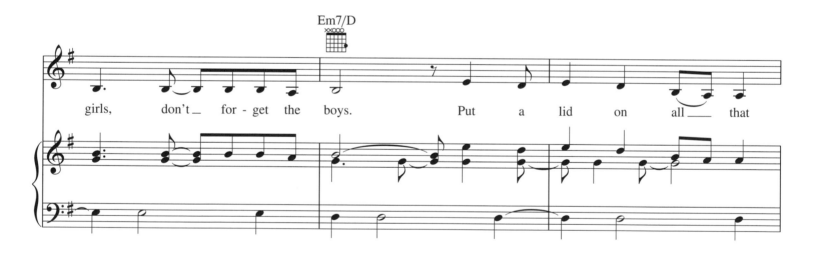

Call _ on all your

girls, don't _ for - get the boys. Put a lid on all _ that

noise. I'm _____

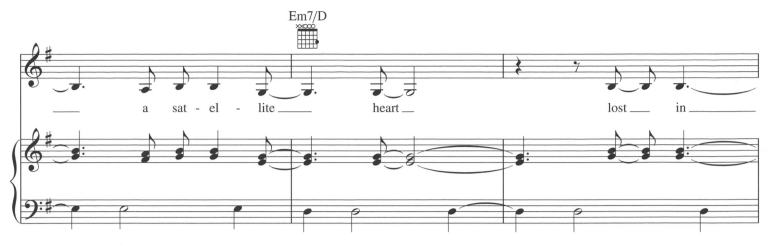

a sat - el - lite ___ heart ___ lost ___ in ___

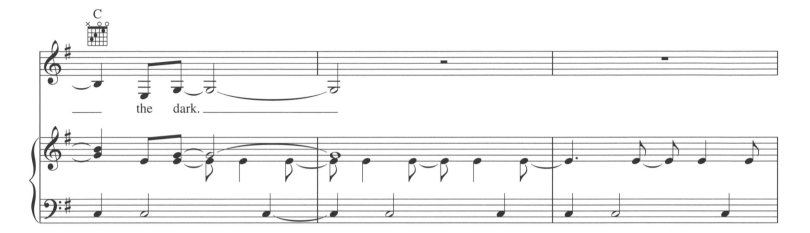

the dark. ___

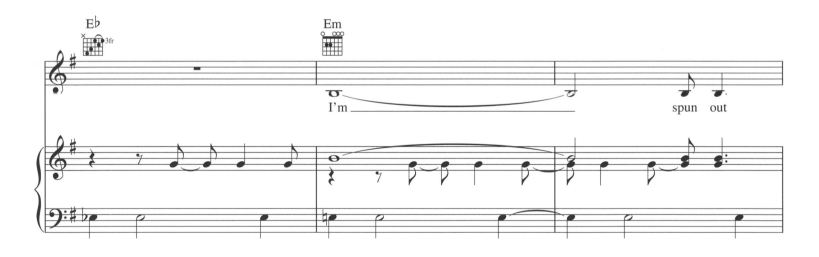

I'm ___ spun out

so far, ___ you ___ stop, I ___ start ___

but I'll _____ be _____ true _____ to

you.

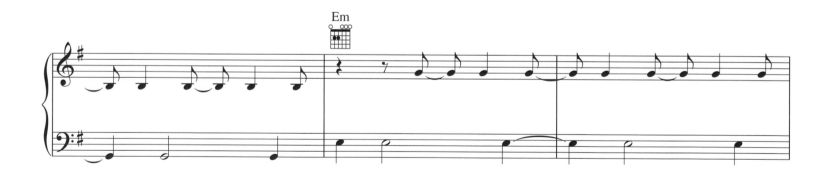

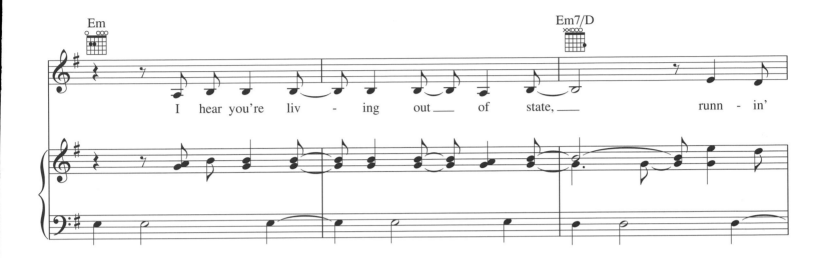

I hear you're liv - ing out ___ of state, ___ runn - in'

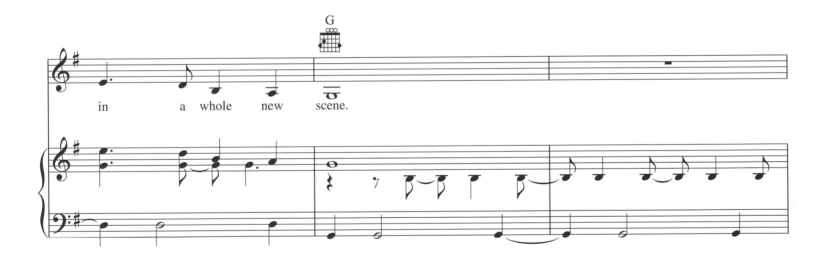

in a whole new scene.

You know, I have - n't slept ___ in weeks. ___ You're the

on - ly thing I _____ see. _____

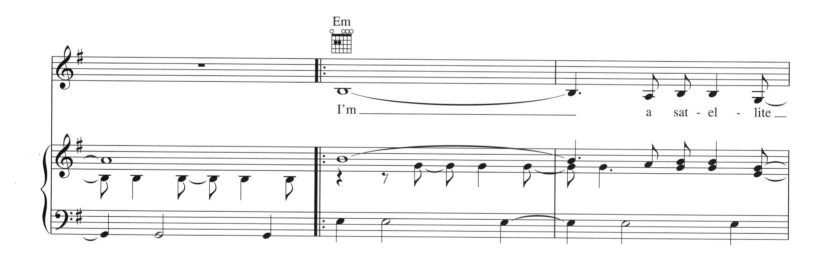

I'm _____ a sat - el - lite ___

___ heart ___ lost ___ in _____ the dark. _____

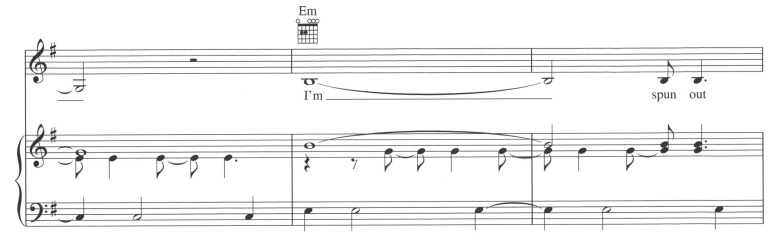

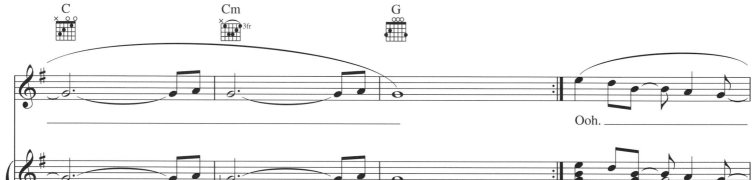

I BELONG TO YOU
(New Moon Remix)

Words and Music by
MATTHEW BELLAMY

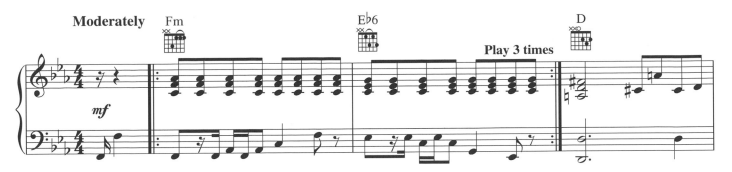

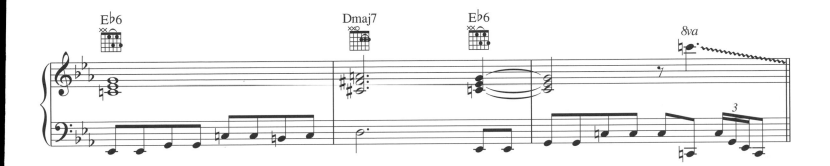

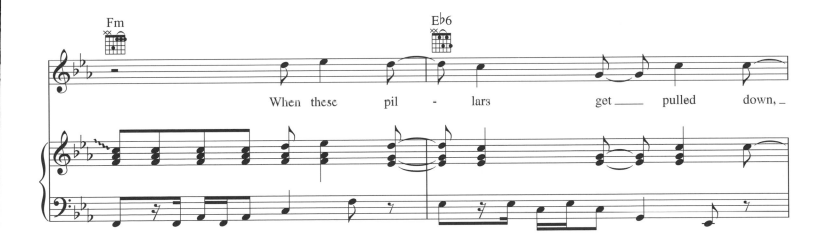

When these pil - lars get ___ pulled down, ___

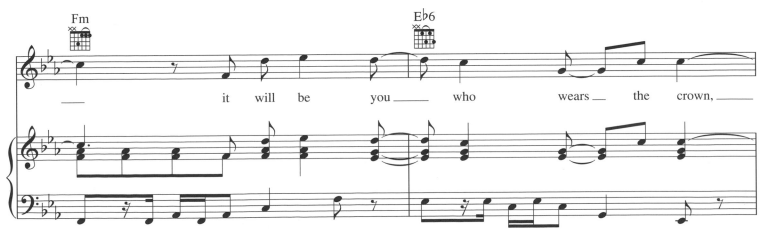

___ it will be you ___ who wears ___ the crown, ___

and I'll owe ev - 'ry - thing __ to you. ___

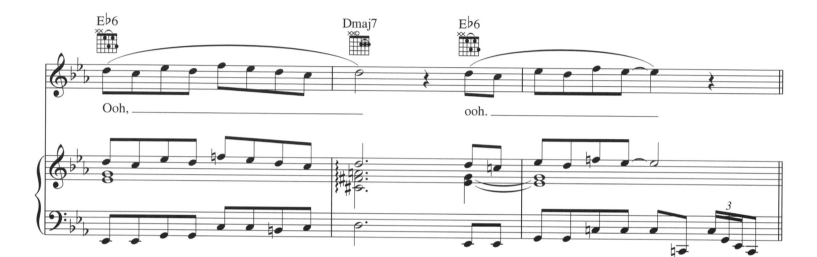

Ooh, _____ ooh. _____

How much pain _____ has cracked __ your soul? __
Then she at - tacks _____ me like a Le - o ___

How much love _____ would make __ you whole? _____
when my heart _____ is split like Ri - o, _____

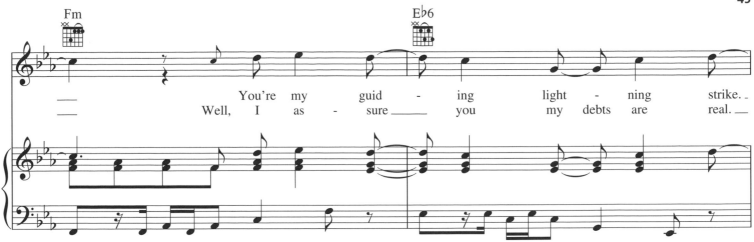

You're my guid - ing light - ning strike.
Well, I as - sure you my debts are real.

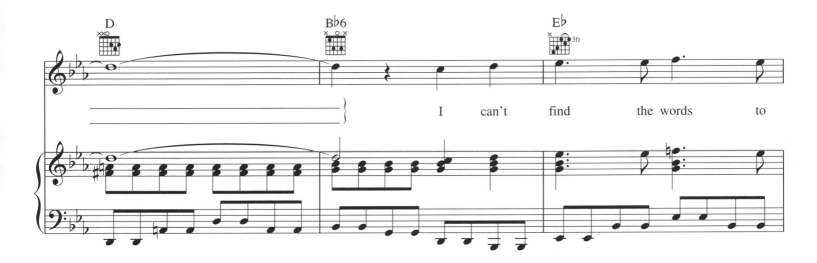

I can't find the words to

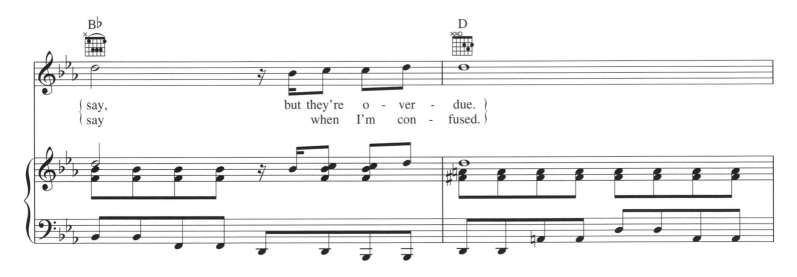

say,
say
but they're o - ver - due.
when I'm con - fused.

I've trav - eled half the world to say
I be - long to
you are my

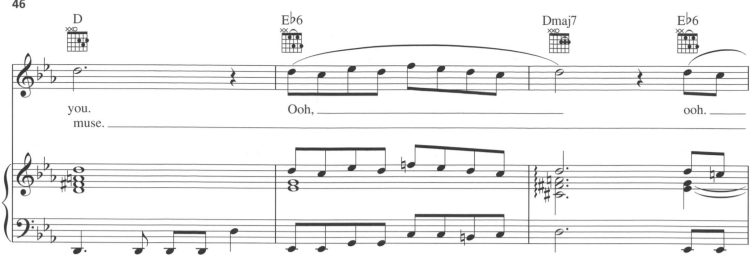

you.
muse.
Ooh,
ooh.

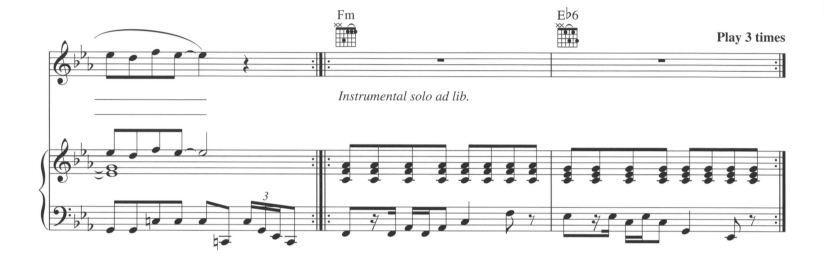

Instrumental solo ad lib.

Play 3 times

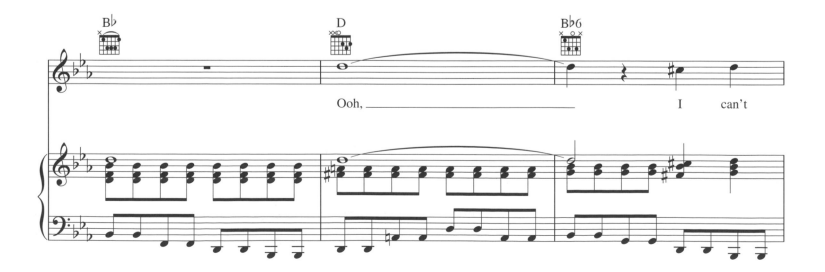

Ooh,
I can't

find the words to say, but they're o - ver -

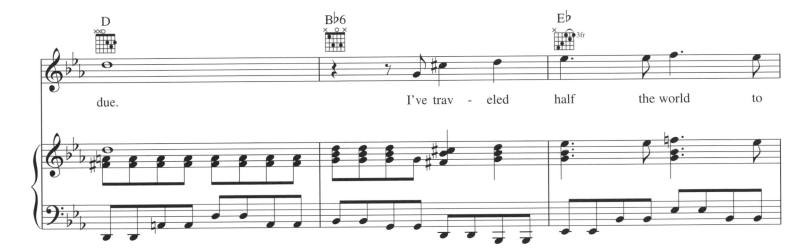

due. I've trav - eled half the world to

say I be-long to you. Ooh, _____

_____ ooh. _____

ROSLYN

Words and Music by
JUSTIN VERNON

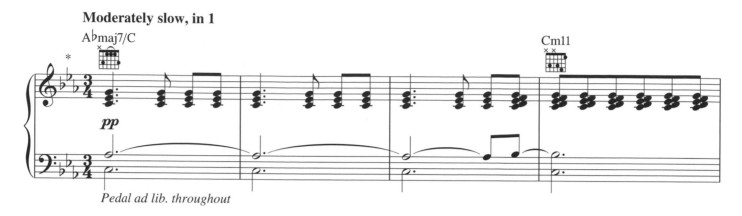

Pedal ad lib. throughout

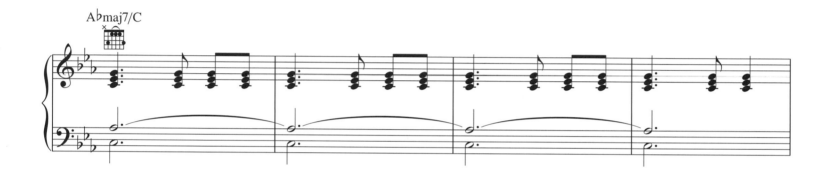

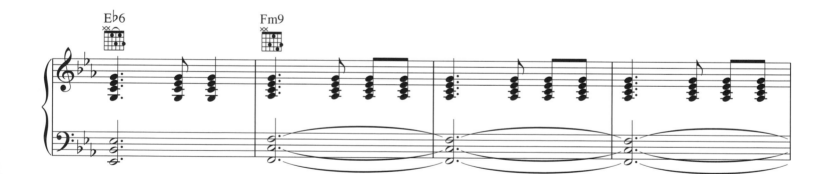

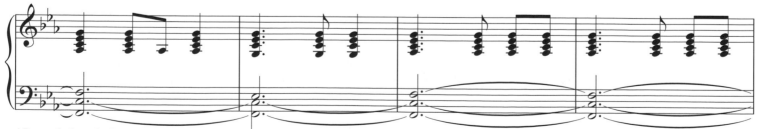

Recorded a whole step lower.

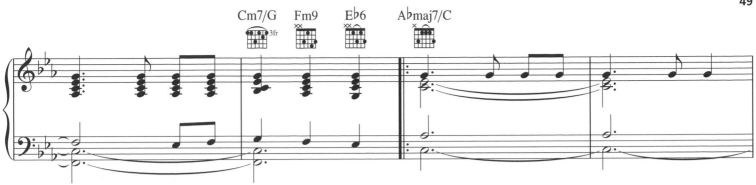

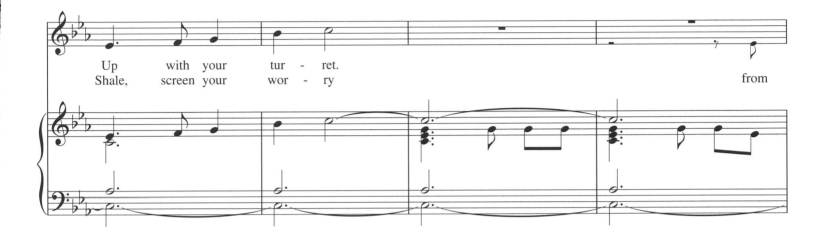

Up   with your   tur - ret.
Shale,   screen your   wor - ry

from

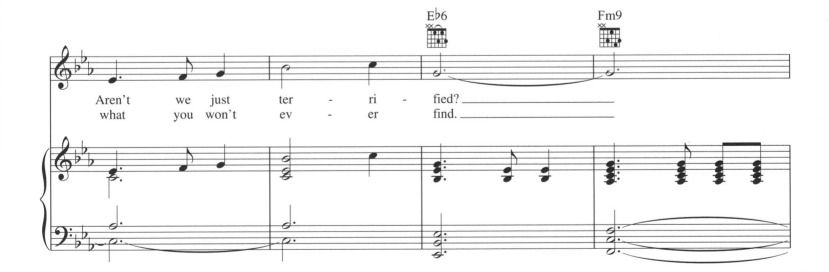

Aren't   we   just   ter - ri - fied? _____
what   you   won't   ev - er   find. _____

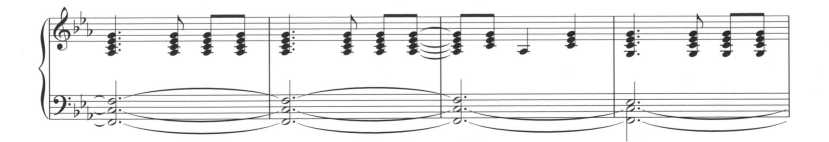

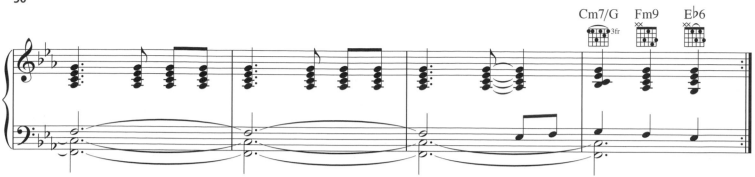

Don't   let   it   fool   you.
Wings   would-n't help   you.

Don't _____ let it ____ fool ____ you...
Wings _____ would - n't ____ help ____ you...

down. _____
down. _____

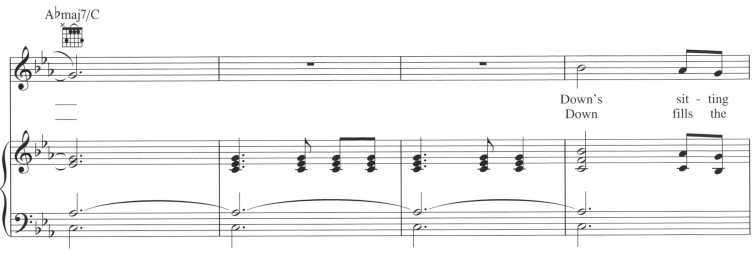

Down's   sit - ting
Down   fills   the

round, _____
ground, _____

folds   in the
grav - i - ty's

gown. _____
proud. _____

To Coda ⊕

Sea and the rock be - low, ___
Bones, blood and teeth e - rode ___

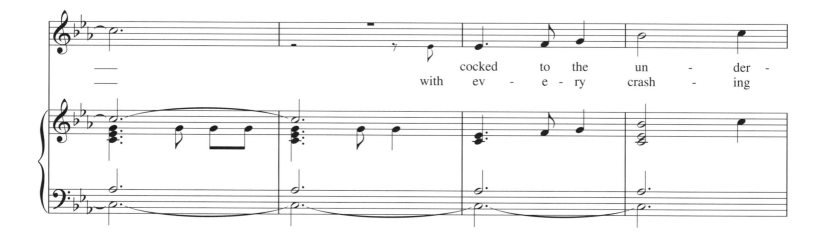

___ cocked to the un - der - ing
___ with ev - e - ry crash - ing

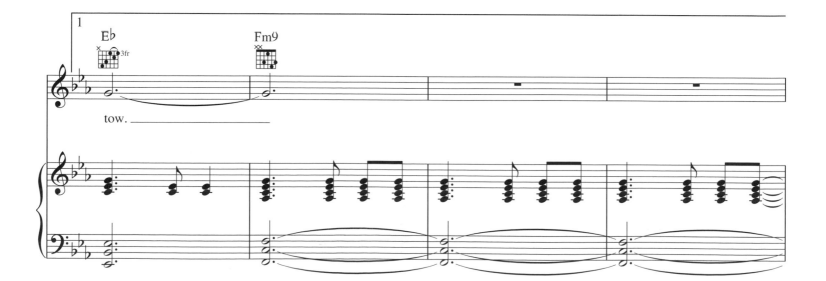

tow. ___

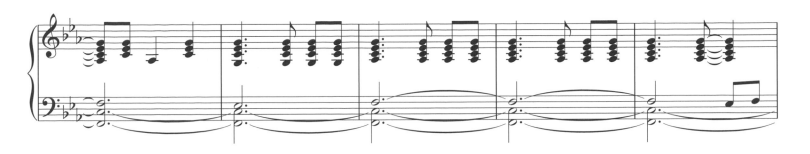

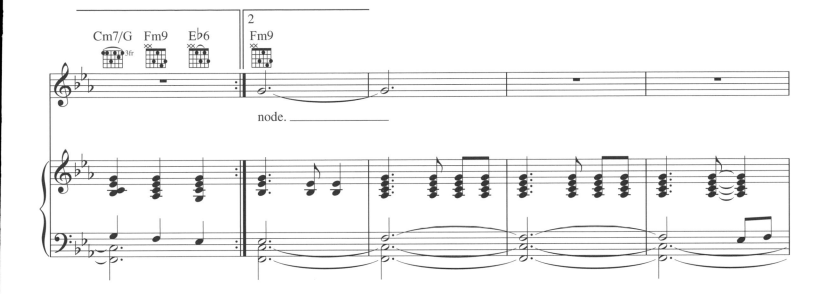

node.

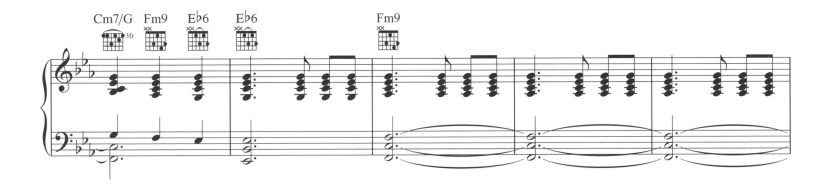

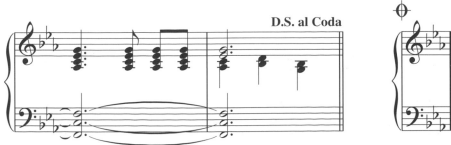

D.S. al Coda

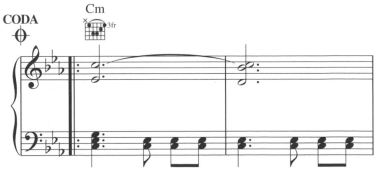

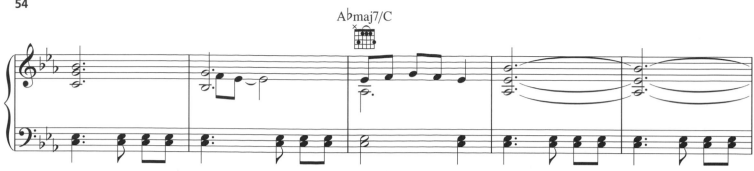

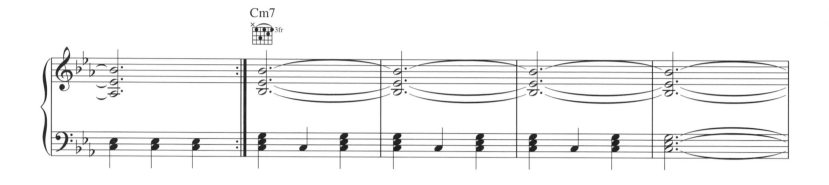

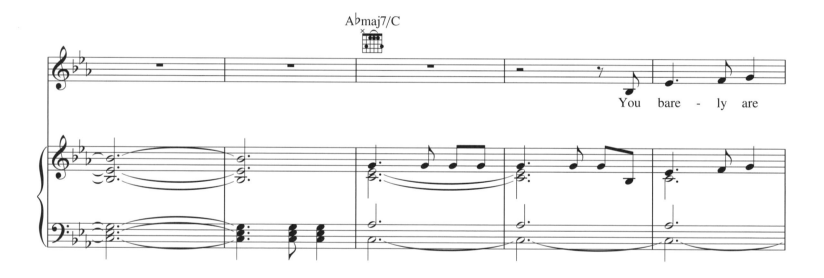

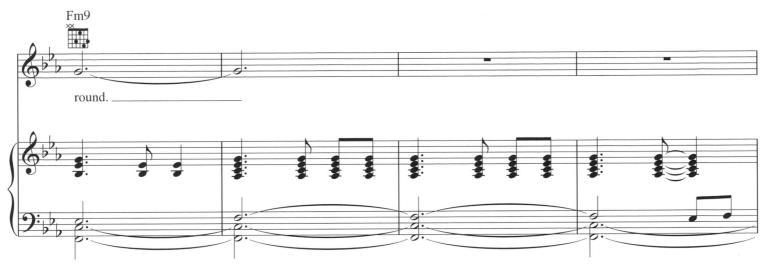

round. _____

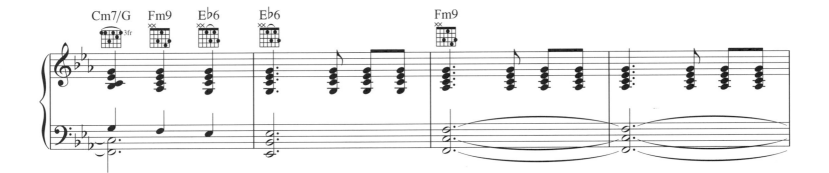

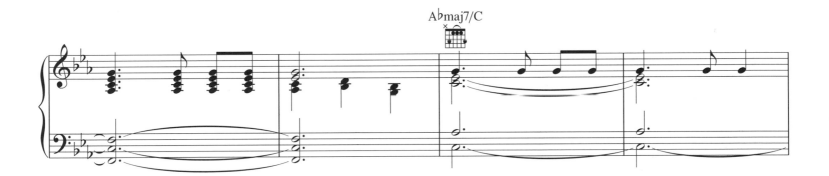

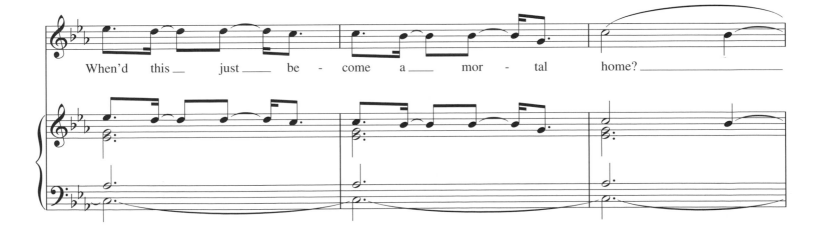

When'd this ___ just ___ be - come a ___ mor - tal home? _____

Nev - er, _____ ooh. _____

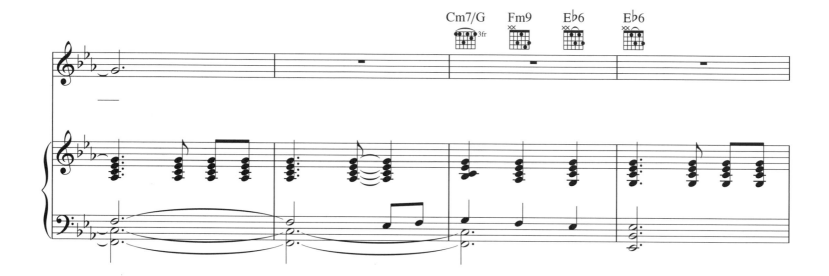

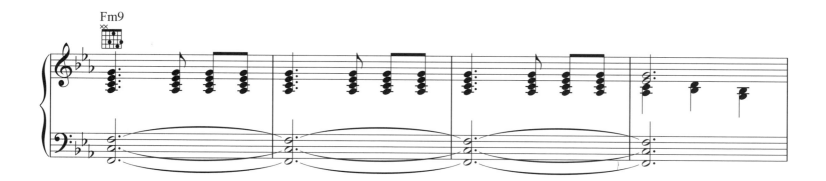

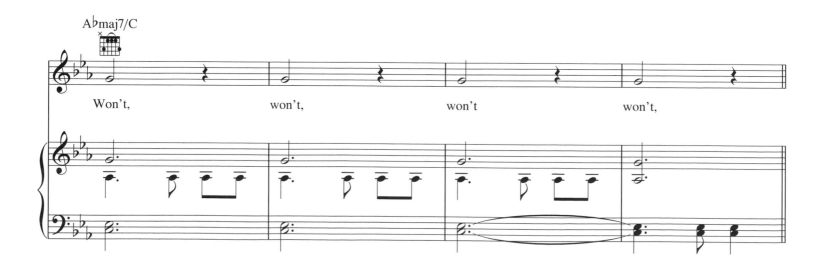

Won't, won't, won't won't,

won't   let   you ____ talk   me, _____
won't   let   you ____ talk   me... _____

down. _____

DONE ALL WRONG

Words and Music by PETER HAYES
and ROBERT BEEN

I done me wrong,_____ I done all
wrong,_____ if you done all

wrong.
wrong,

All the wrong I done,_ I'm sure to live_ quite_
you can rest as - sured_ you're gon - na live_ quite_

(Solo ends)   We're do - ing

wrong, _____ we all done ___ wrong.   If we

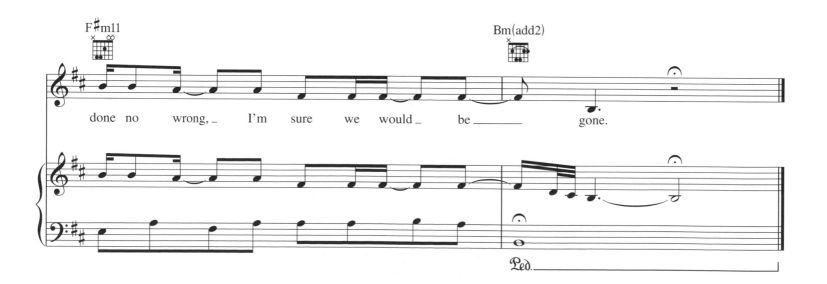

done no   wrong, _   I'm   sure   we   would _   be _____   gone.

MONSTERS

Words and Music by
STEVE SCHLITZ

Moderately fast

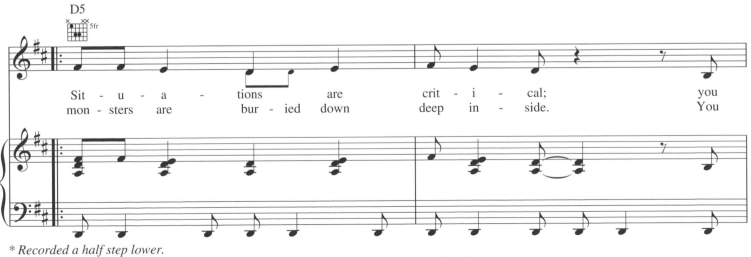

Sit - u - a - tions are crit - i - cal; you

mon - sters are bur - ied down deep in - side. You

* Recorded a half step lower.

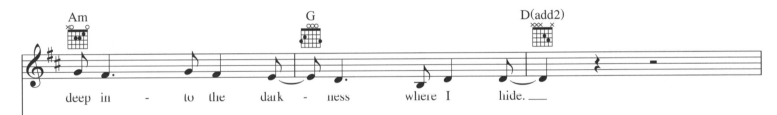

To Coda ⊕

- ness where I hide. ___

Guitar solo ad lib.

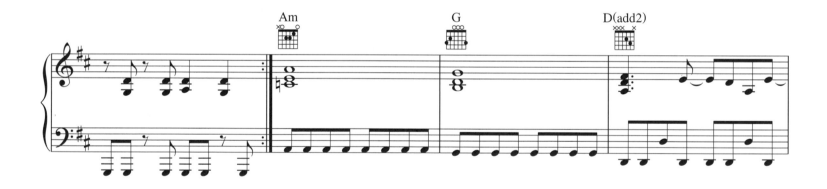

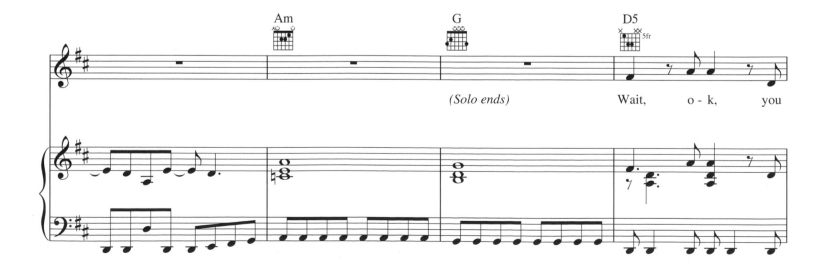

(Solo ends) Wait, o - k, you

D.S. al Coda

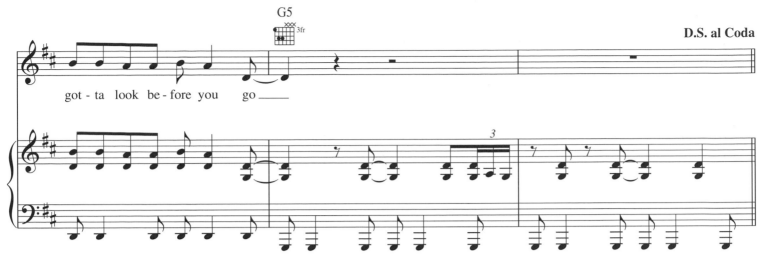

got - ta look be - fore you go ____

CODA

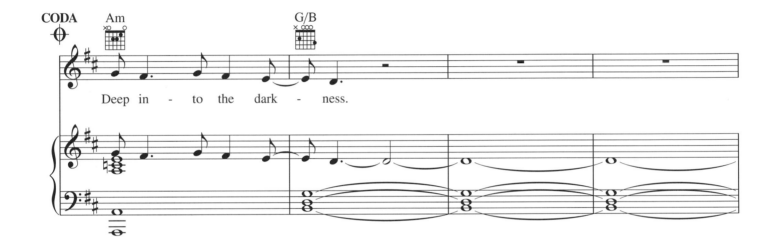

Deep in - to the dark - ness.

THE VIOLET HOUR

Words and Music by
ALEX BROWN CHURCH

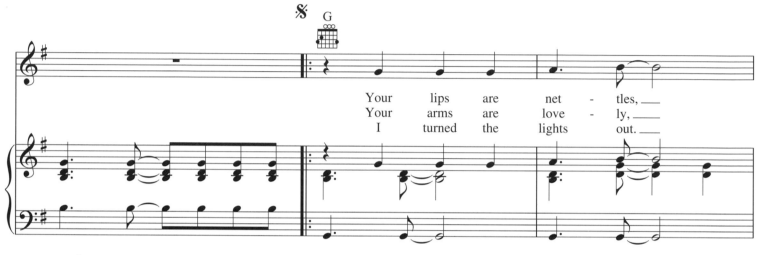

Your lips are net - tles, _____
Your arms are love - ly, _____
I turned the lights out. _____

your tongue is wine. _____ Your laugh - ter's
yel - low and rose. _____ Your back's a
I cleaned the sheets. _____ You changed the

li - quid _____ but your bod - y's pine.
mead - ow _____ cov - ered in snow.
sta - tion, _____ turned up the heat.

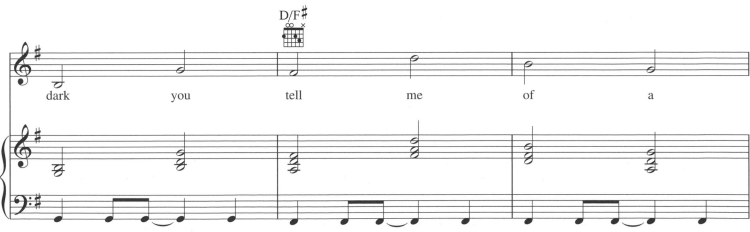

flow - er _____

that on - ly blooms _____

in the vio - let hour. _____

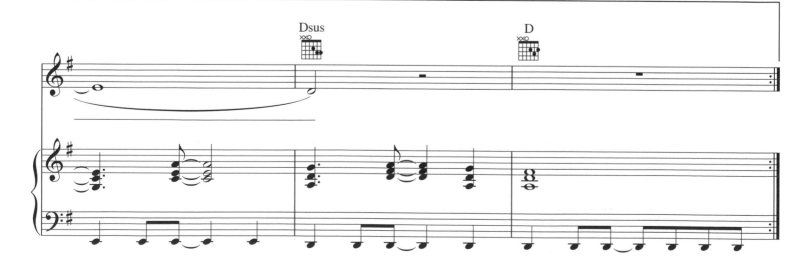

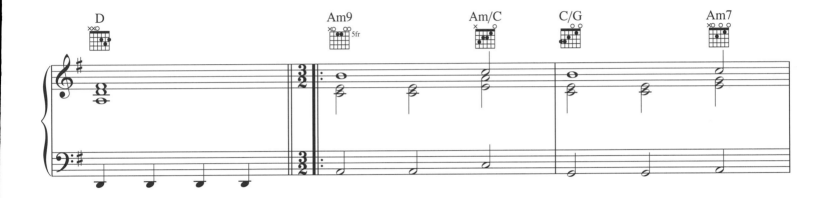

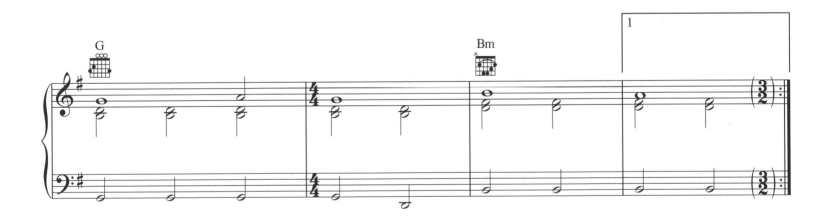

D.S. al Coda

CODA

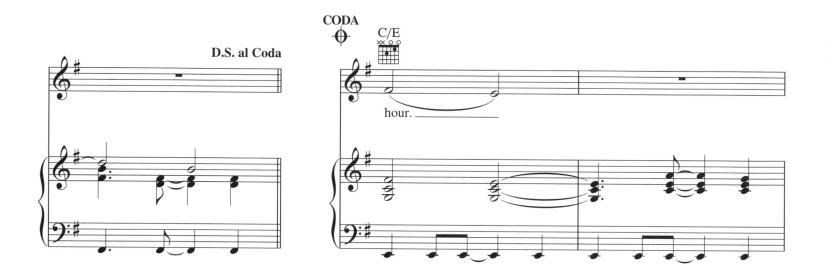

hour. _____

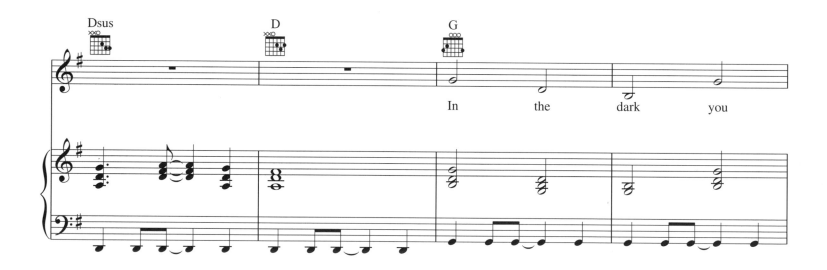

In the dark you

tell me of a flow - er _____

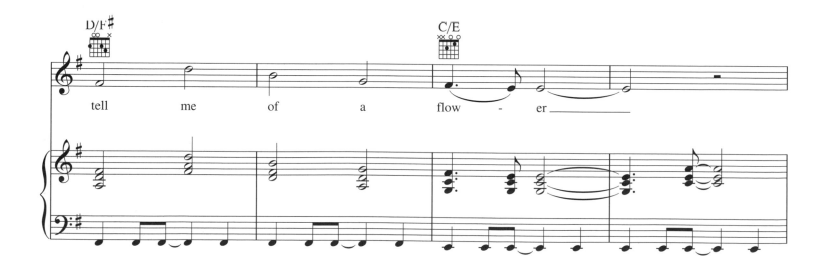

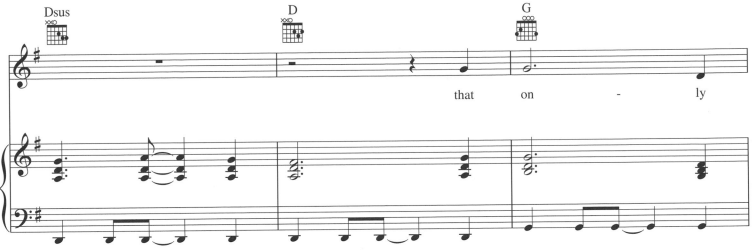

that on - ly

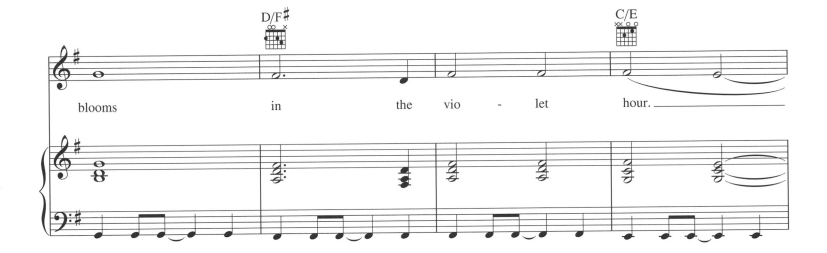

blooms   in   the   vio - let   hour. _____

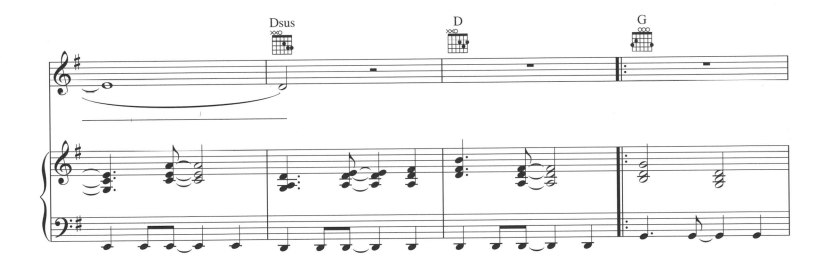

Play 4 times

SHOOTING THE MOON

Words and Music by DAMIAN KULASH
and TIM NORDWIND

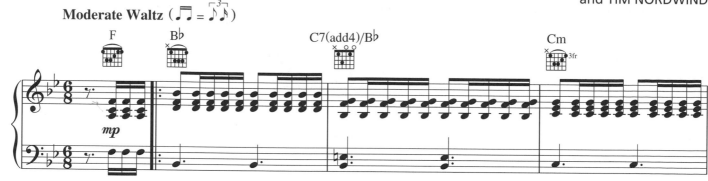

All of the as-tro-nauts, cham-pagne in
prin-ci-pals, gen-'rals

plas-tic cups, wait-ing for the big her-o to show. _____ Out-side the
ad-mir-als and the pod-i-um lit with a spot-light The crowd buzz-ing

door he stands, his head in his hands and his heart in his throat.
qui-et-ly, wait-ing ex-pec-tant-ly like it's op-en-ing night.

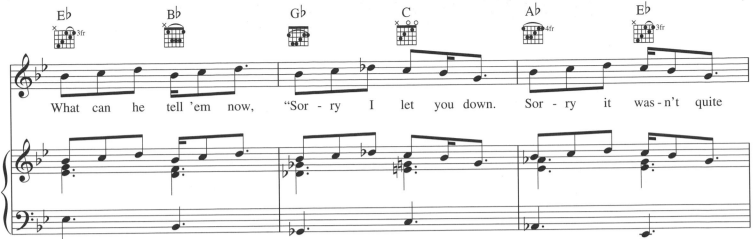

What can he tell 'em now, "Sor - ry I let you down. Sor - ry it was - n't quite

true. __ But don't get hung up on it, just sold - ier on __ with it and

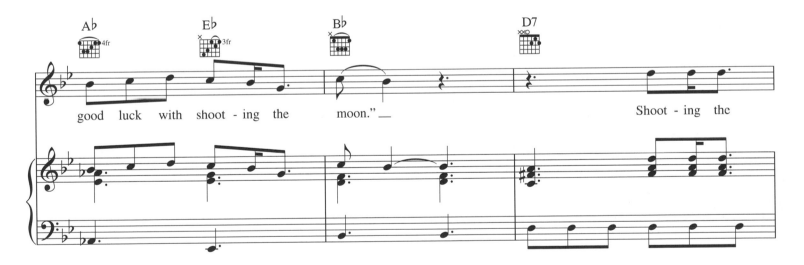

good luck with shoot - ing the moon." __ Shoot - ing the

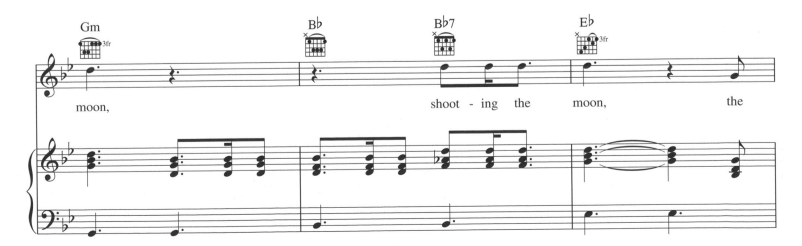

moon, shoot - ing the moon, the

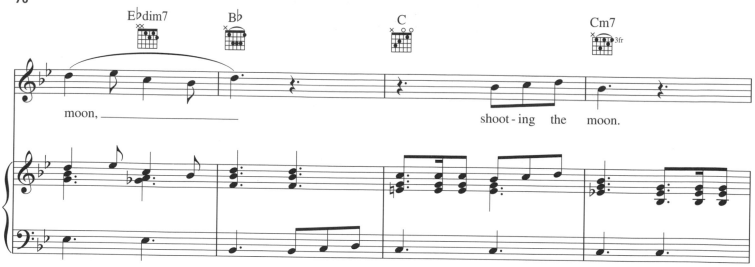

moon, _____

shoot - ing the moon.

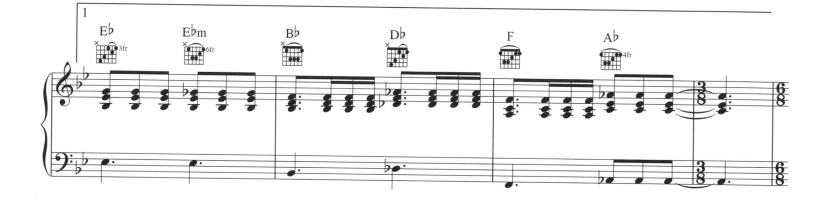

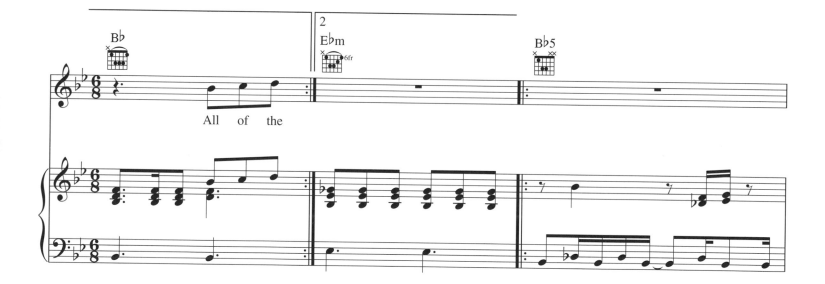

All of the

Play 4 times

SLOW LIFE

Words and Music by
GRIZZLY BEAR

I think __ I know __ what's on __ your mind, __
__ you want __ it's fine. __

a cou - ple words
Keep all __ the slow __

__ a great di - vide. __
__ life bor - der - line.

*Recorded a half step lower.

Place your bets on chance and a - pa - thy. ___

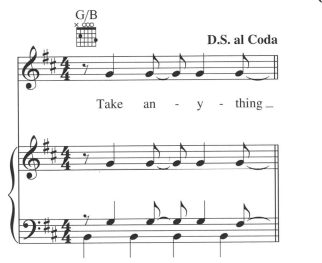

D.S. al Coda

Take an - y - thing ___

CODA

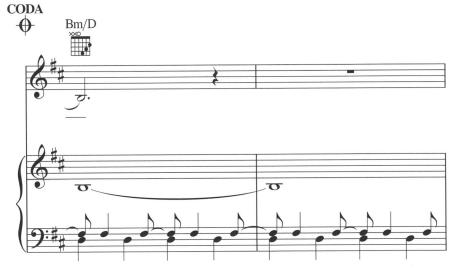

Ev - en though you're the on - ly one ___ I see, ___ it's the

last ca - tas - tro - phe.___ Place your bets on chance and a - pa - thy, __

___ time to win this o - pen - ly.___ Ev - en though you're the

___ Ev - en though you're the on - ly one___ I see.___

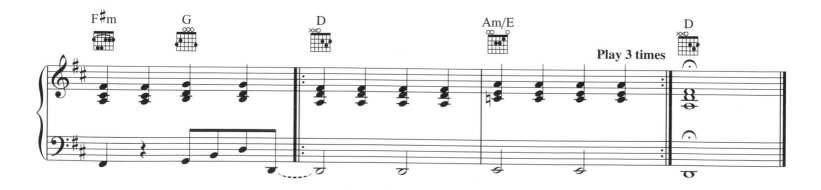

Play 3 times

NO SOUND BUT THE WIND

Words and Music by TOM SMITH,
CHRIS URBANOWICZ, RUSSELL LEETCH
and ED LAY

Moderately, with feeling

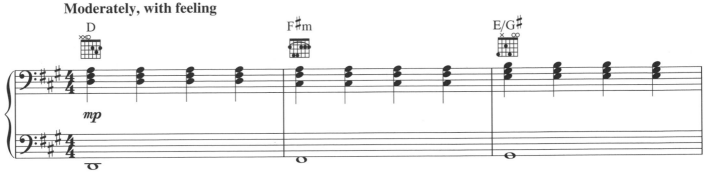

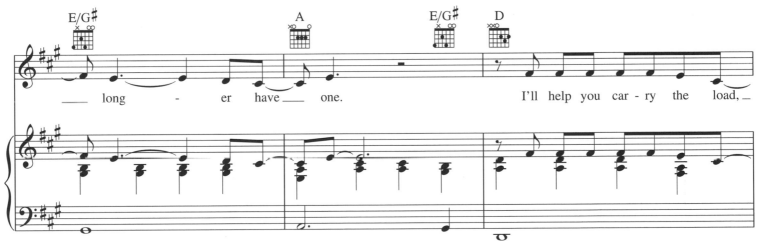

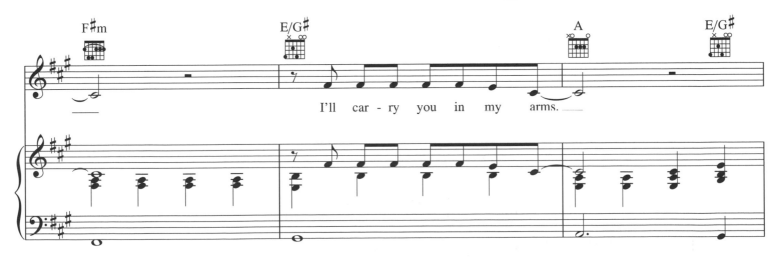

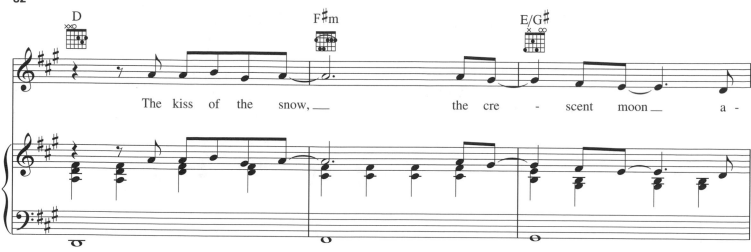

The kiss of the snow, ___ the cre - scent moon ___ a -

bove us. ___ Our blood is cold ___ and we're a - lone ___

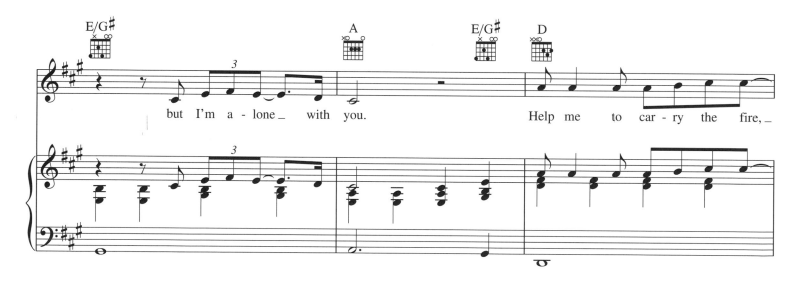

but I'm a - lone _ with you. Help me to car - ry the fire, __

we will keep it a - light _____ to - geth - er. ___

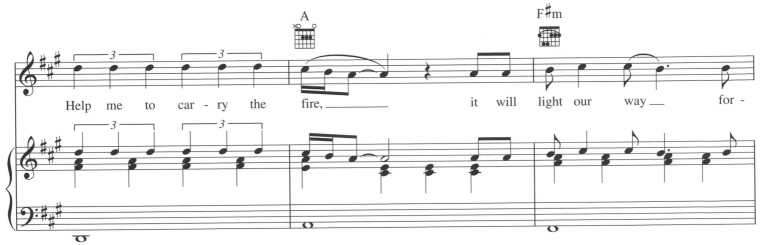

Help me to car - ry the fire, _____ it will light our way ___ for -

ev - er. If I say shut your eyes, ___

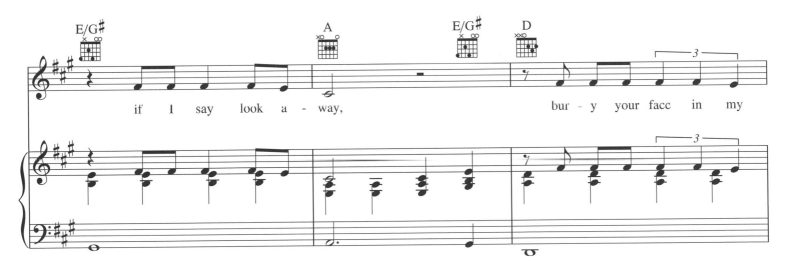

if I say look a - way, bur - y your face in my

should - er, ___ think of a birth - day. ___

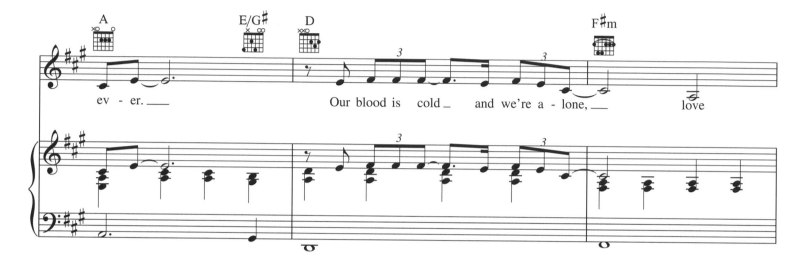

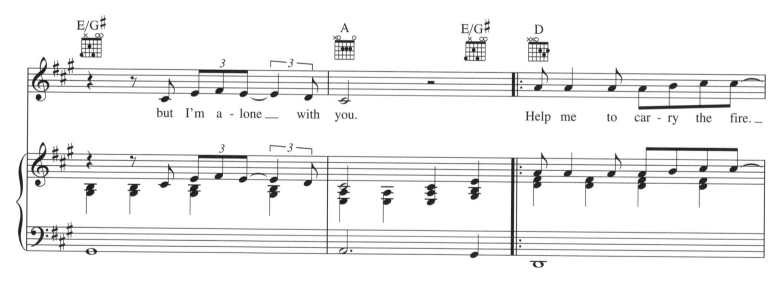

Help me to car - ry the fire, _____ it will { light our way ___ for - for -
{ light up our way

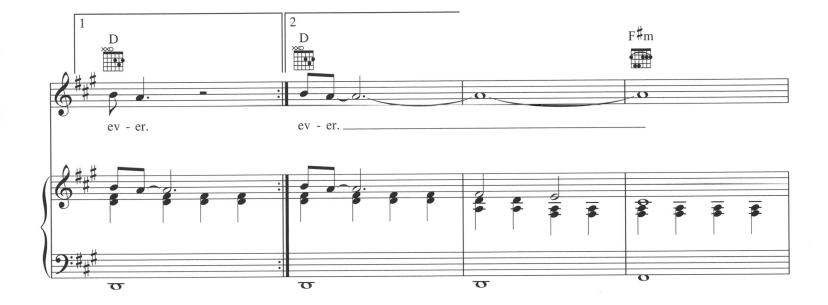

1 ev - er.   2 ev - er. _____

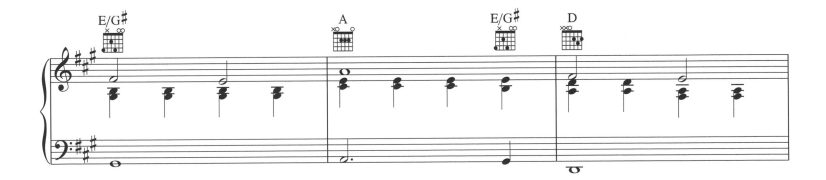

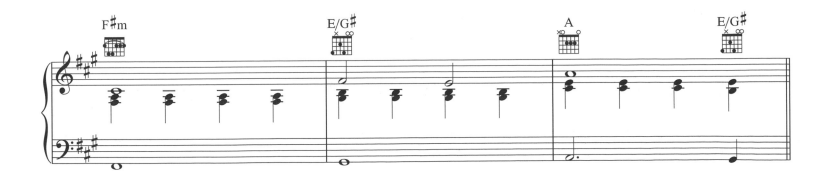

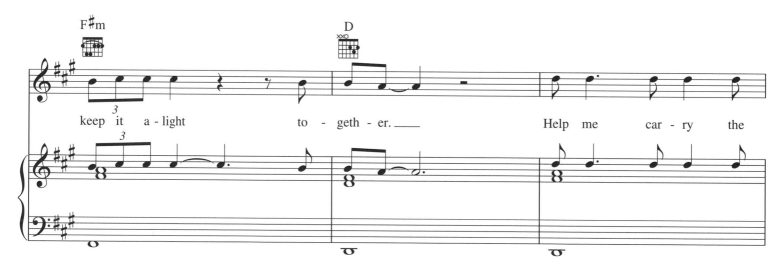

NEW MOON
(The Meadow)

Composed by
ALEXANDRE DESPLAT

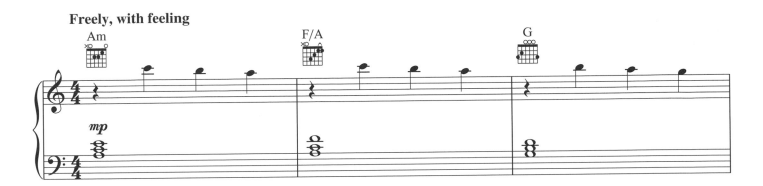

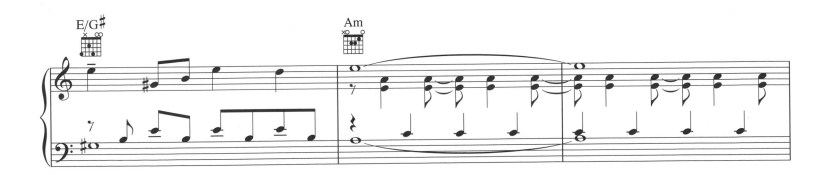

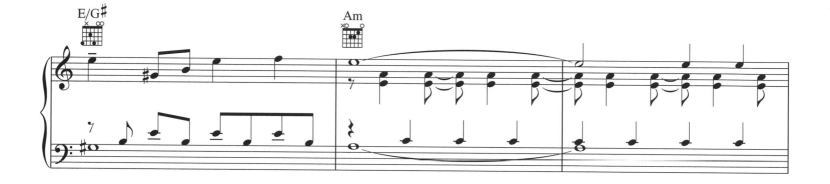

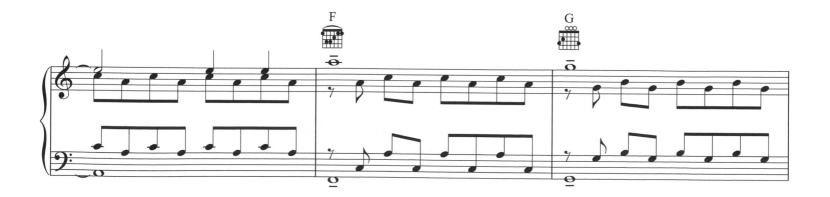

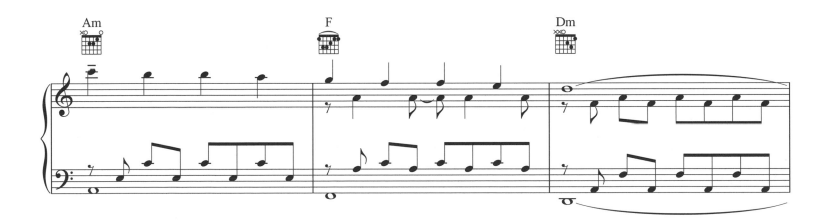

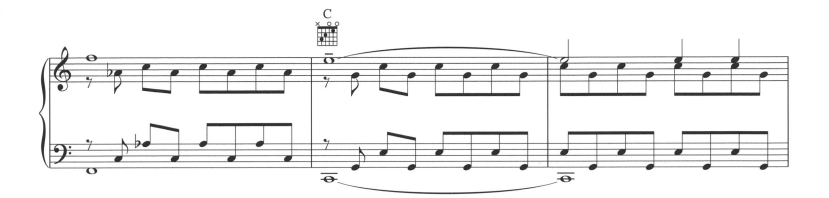

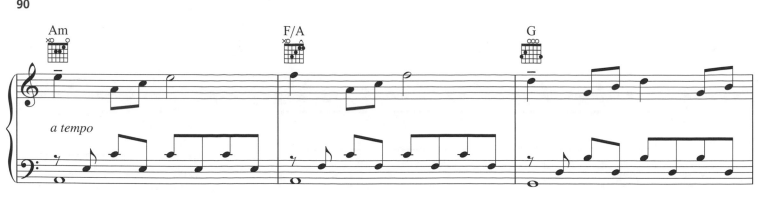

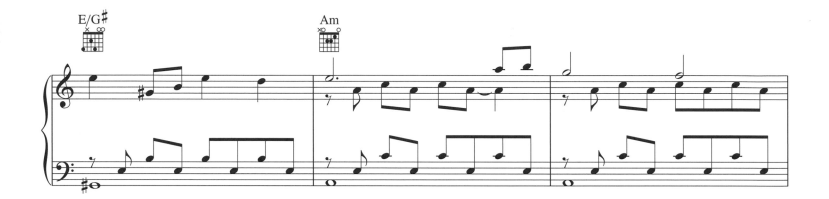

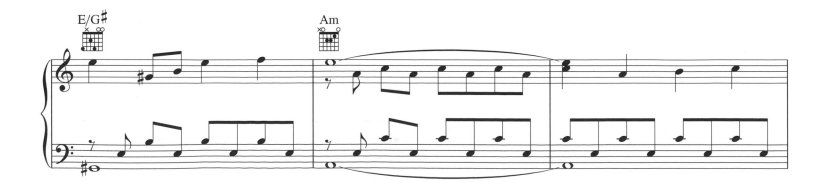

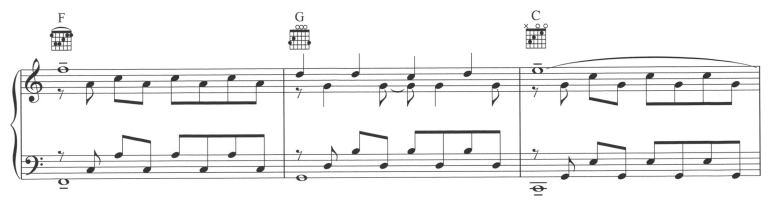

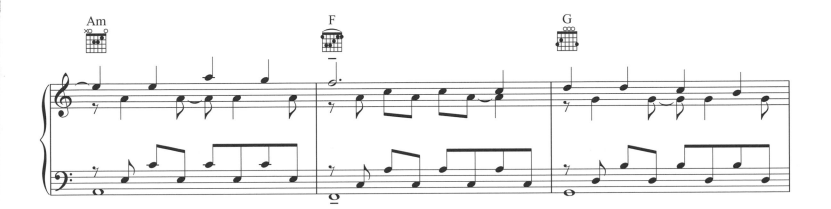

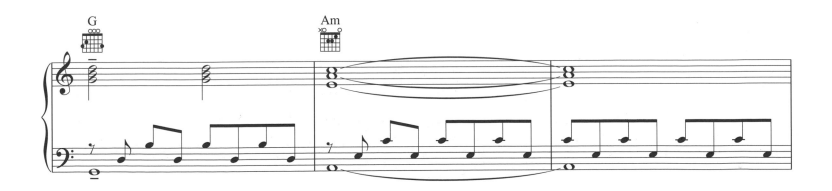

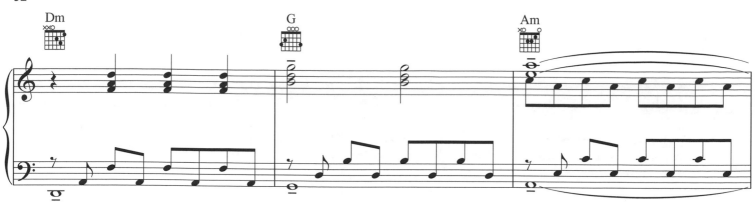

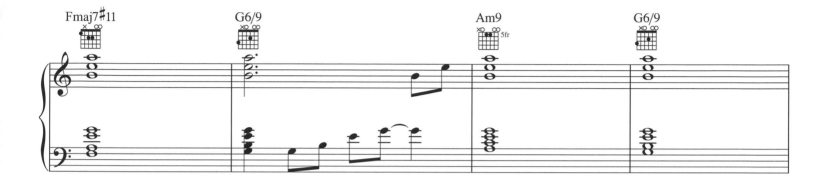

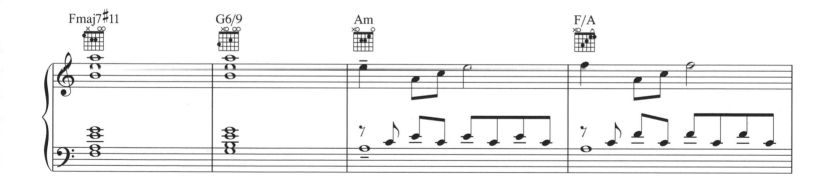

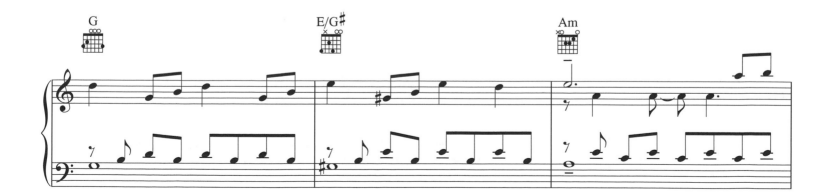

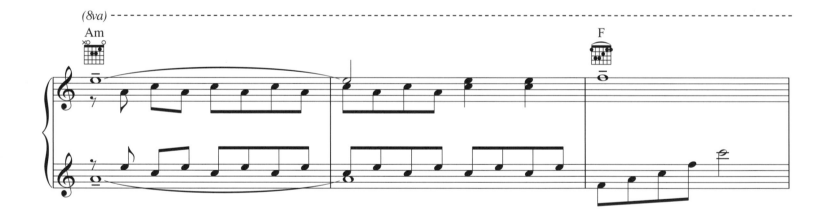

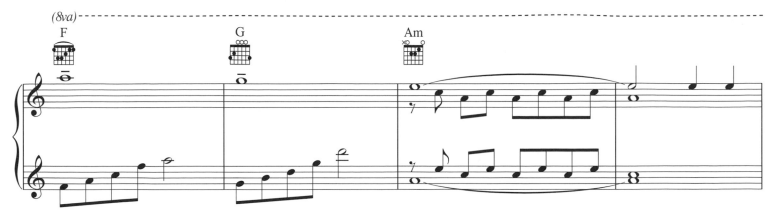

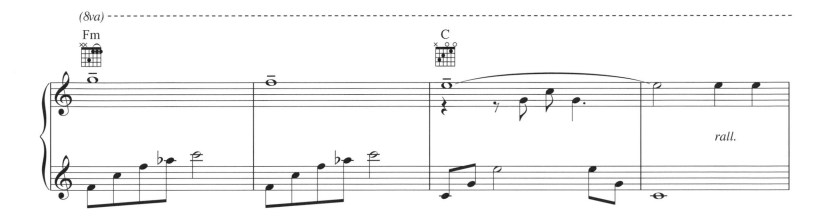

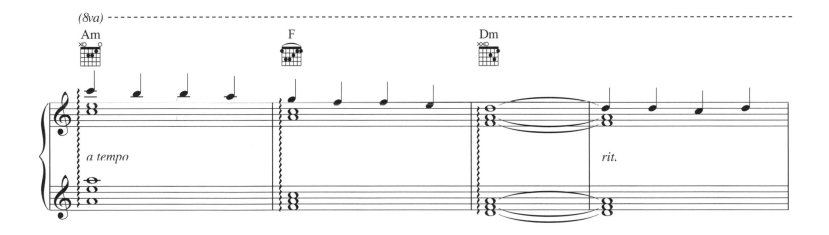

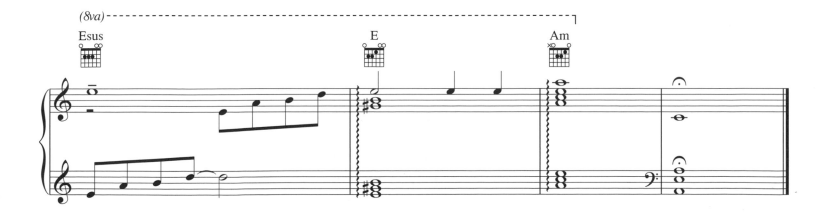